I0407695

The Book of
GRATITUDE

801 Quotes to Build a Happier Life

James Allen Proctor

Table of Contents

Published by FastForwardPublishing.com

Copyright © 2017 by FastForwardPublishing All rights reserved.

Permission to reproduce or transmit in any form or by any means, electronic or mechanical, including photocopying and recording, or by any information storage or retrieval system, must be obtained in writing from FastForward Publishing.

This book has been fully researched for factual accuracy. The authors and publishers cannot assume responsibility for any errors or omissions. The reader assumes all responsibilities for any loss or damages, whether consequential, incidental or otherwise that may result from the information presented in this publication.

We rely on our experience and thorough research processes to determine that the information presented in this book is as factual and well thought out as possible. In the event that any material is incorrect or not appropriately attributed, please contact us and we will make any necessary changes or additions, as quickly as possible.

Please feel free to share this book with family and friends. If you feel others may benefit from this book, you can make them aware of how to access the book so they can download a copy if they so choose.

ISBN-13: 978-1542853958
ISBN-10: 1542853958

Foreward

The idea of keeping a positive attitude has always made sense to me. And, I was pretty good at keeping my attitude positive by following a simple two-step process: **Think About It + Feel Good About It.**

When I added gratitude into the process, it ramped up my positive attitude by keeping me focused on the abundance in my life: **Think About It + Feel Good About It + Be Thankful For It**. The contents of this book will help you see how adding gratitude can ramp it up for you, too.

A few years ago, I took it to the next level by starting to make daily entries into a gratitude journal. Not only did this new process make me happier, but it also helped me reduce stress. Here's my simple "formula" in its current, very effective state:

**Think About It + Feel Good About It +
Be Thankful For It + Write It Down**

The quotes in this book are here to help you stay on track, to remind you of the benefits of practicing gratitude and to motivate you to keep taking it to the next level. It's worked for me, I sincerely hope they resonate with you.

> NOTE: If you feel like you're ready to start keeping a gratitude journal, you can get the same one I use by going to your favorite online book retailer and searching "gratitude journal James Allen Proctor."

Recommended Books

James Allen Proctor's
The Gratitude Journal,
A perfect "partner" for
The Book of Gratitude.
Strengthen your spirit
with this simple journal
that offers a framework
for practicing the power
of gratitude each day,
while keeping a record
of your blessings for
future inspiration.

Achieve greater levels of success with one or both
of these personal growth manuals

Introduction
E.K. Mason

How Gratitude Can Change Your Life

Gratitude means thankfulness, counting your blessings, noticing simple pleasures, and acknowledging everything that you receive. It means learning to live your life as if everything were a miracle, and being aware on a continuous basis of how much you've been given. Gratitude shifts your focus from what your life lacks to the abundance that is already present. In addition, behavioral and psychological research has shown the surprising life improvements that can stem from the practice of gratitude. Giving thanks makes people happier and more resilient, it strengthens relationships, it improves health, and it reduces stress.

Research Shows Gratitude Heightens Quality of Life

Two psychologists, Michael McCollough of Southern Methodist University in Dallas, Texas, and Robert Emmons of the University of California at Davis, wrote an article about an experiment they conducted on gratitude and its impact on well-being. The study split several hundred people into three different groups and all of the participants were asked to keep daily diaries. The first group kept a diary of the events that occurred during the day without being told specifically to write about either good or bad things; the second group was told to record their unpleasant experiences; and the last group was instructed to make a daily list of things for which they were grateful. The results of the study indicated that daily gratitude exercises resulted in higher reported levels of alertness, enthusiasm, determination, optimism, and energy. In addition, those in the **gratitude** group experienced less depression and stress, were more likely to help others, exercised more regularly, and made greater progress toward achieving personal goals.

Dr. Emmons – who has been studying gratitude for almost ten years and is considered by many to be the world's leading authority on gratitude – is author of the book, *Thanks!: How the New Science of Gratitude Can Make You Happier*. The information in this book is based on research involving thousands of people conducted by a number of different researchers around the world. One of the things these studies show is that practicing gratitude can increase happiness levels by around 25%. This is significant, among other things, because just as there's a certain weight that feels natural to your body and which your body strives to maintain, your basic level of happiness is set at a predetermined point. If something bad happens to you during the day, your happiness can drop momentarily, but then it returns to its natural set-point. Likewise, if something positive happens to you, your level of happiness rises, and then it returns once again to your "happiness set-point". A practice of gratitude raises your "happiness set-point" so you can remain at a higher level of happiness regardless of outside circumstances.

In addition, Dr. Emmons' research shows that those who practice gratitude tend to be more creative, bounce back more quickly from adversity, have a stronger immune system, and have stronger social relationships than those who don't practice gratitude. He further points out that "To say we feel grateful is not to say that everything in our lives is necessarily great. It just means we are aware of our blessings."

Notice and Appreciate Each Day's Gifts

People tend to take for granted the good that is already present in their lives. There's a gratitude exercise that instructs that you should imagine losing some of the things that you take for granted, such as your home, your ability to see or hear, your ability to walk, or anything that currently gives you comfort. Then imagine getting each of these things back, one by one, and consider how grateful you would be for each and every one. In addition, you need to start finding joy in the small things instead of holding out for big achievements-such as getting the promotion, having a comfortable nest egg saved up, getting married, having the baby, and so on–before allowing yourself to feel gratitude and joy.

Another way to use giving thanks to appreciate life more fully is to use gratitude to help you put things in their proper perspective. When things don't go your way, remember that every difficulty carries within it the seeds of an equal or greater benefit. In the face of adversity ask yourself: "What's good about this?", "What can I learn from this?", and "How can I benefit from this?"

There are Many Ways to Practice Gratitude

A common method to develop the practice of gratitude is to keep a gratitude **journal**, a concept that was made famous by Sarah Ban Breathnach's book *Simple Abundance Journal of Gratitude*. This exercise basically consists of writing down every day a list of three to ten things for which you are grateful; you can do this first thing in the morning or before going to bed at night. Another exercise you can try is to write a gratitude letter to a person who has exerted a positive influence in your life but whom you have not properly thanked. Some experts suggest that you set up a meeting with this person and read the letter to them face to face.

Last year millions of people took the challenge proposed by Will Bowen, a Kansas City minister, to go 21 days without complaining, criticizing, or gossiping. To help condition the participants to stop complaining, they each wore a purple No-Complaint wristband. Several authors in the self-improvement genre have suggested that people do something similar to help condition themselves to be constantly aware of the things in life that they're grateful for.

A variation of the wristband concept is to create a gratitude charm bracelet, with either one meaningful charm or different charms representing the things you're most grateful for. For example, you could have a charm shaped like a heart to symbolize your significant other, figurines to represent different family members, an apple to represent health, a dollar sign to symbolize abundance, a charm that represents your current profession or a future career, and maybe a charm that makes you laugh to represent humor and joy.

Conclusion

Once you become oriented toward looking for things to be grateful for, you will find that you begin to appreciate simple pleasures and things that you previously took for granted. Gratitude should not be just a reaction to getting what you want, but an all-the-time gratitude, the kind where you notice the little things and where you constantly look for the good even in unpleasant situations. Today, start bringing gratitude to your experiences, instead of waiting for a positive experience in order to feel grateful; in this way, you'll be on your way toward becoming a master of gratitude.

= = = = = =

E.K. Mason is the author of *Change Your Thinking and Your Life Will Follow: Adjust Your Mental Focus to Support Achievement*

CHANGE YOUR THINKING
— and —
YOUR LIFE WILL FOLLOW

Adjusting Your Mental Focus
to Support Achievement

E. K. Mason

Be Thankful

Be thankful that you don't already have everything you desire,
If you did, what would there be to look forward to?

Be thankful when you don't know something
For it gives you the opportunity to learn.

Be thankful for the difficult times.
During those times you grow.

Be thankful for your limitations
Because they give you opportunities for improvement.

Be thankful for each new challenge
Because it will build your strength and character.

Be thankful for your mistakes
They will teach you valuable lessons.

Be thankful when you're tired and weary
Because it means you've made a difference.

It is easy to be thankful for the good things.
A life of rich fulfillment comes to those who are
also thankful for the setbacks.

Gratitude can turn a negative into a positive.
Find a way to be thankful for your troubles
and they can become your blessings.

The Quotes

"Gratitude is one of the virtues of the noble man. It is the hallmark of a life lived well. It is a trademark of the righteous man. It is an attribute that significantly impacts on your personal happiness and how sound your relationship will be with others."
- Sesan Kareem

"The true poetic feeling is
a feeling of boundless gratitude."
- Marty Rubin

"Let us rise up and be thankful, for if we didn't learn a lot today, at least we learned a little, and if we didn't learn a little, at least we didn't get sick, and if we got sick, at least we didn't die;
so, let us all be thankful."
- Buddha

"We are all more blind to what we have than to what we have not."
- Audre Lorde

"Eucharisteo-thanksgiving
always precedes the miracle."
- Ann Voskamp

"Some people grumble that roses have thorns; I am grateful that thorns have roses."

Alphonse Karr

"For those who praise God and say "God is good,"
or, 'I'm so blessed," when you get what YOU want,
try praising Him and saying, "God is good," and
"I'm so blessed," when you're suffering. To do the
first is effortless. The masses do it, that's how easy it
is. To do the latter requires something greater:
strength, faith and gratitude - no matter
the ouch involved."
- **Donna Lynn Hope**

"Just as thoughts, send out vibrations to which there
is a creative and attractive power, gratitude
stimulates the field of etheric energy that surrounds
you on a subtle level to bring into your life more
of what brings you joy."
- **Genevieve Gerard**

"My prayer is an attitude of pure gratitude for
having the opportunity to experience life on this
earth with all its pain, heartache, worry, and turmoil;
coupled with this gratitude is the thankfulness for
just having the opportunity to have lived. That is
fairly easy on good days but difficult when life
puts rocks and boulders in the road."
- **David W. Earle**

"People are complaining of having rags and not riches, but I find it a blessing just to have rags, to wipe away the dirt and dust that may come in the course of life."
- Anthony Liccione

"When your heart's gratitude comes to the fore, when you become all gratitude, this gratitude is like a flow, a flow of consciousness. When your consciousness is flowing, feel that this gratitude-flow is like a river that is watering the root of the tree and the tree itself. It is always through gratitude that your consciousness-river will grow and water the perfection-tree inside you."
- Sri Chinmoy

"They do not love, that do not show their love."
- William Shakespeare

"I believe the main purpose of life is to accept with gratitude what you've been blessed with so that you may use those gifts to mold yourself into the best person you can possibly be. Learning to discern things of true value from those of little or no worth is part of the process."
- Richelle E. Goodrich

"Gratitude is a vaccine, an antitoxin,
and an antiseptic."
- **John Henry Jowett**

"Feeling grateful is good; showing appreciation to
those you feel grateful to is sublime." - Andy Lacroix
"Each day, each season, each cycle offers something
of beauty. Let us notice and give thanks."
– **Diane Mariechild**

"We should certainly count our blessings, but we
should also make our blessings count."
- **Neal A. Maxwell**

"Much of the oxygen we breathe comes from plants
that died long ago. We can give thanks to these
ancestors of our present-pay foliage, but we can't
give back to them. We can, however, give forward.
When we are unable to return the favor, we can pay
it forward to someone or something else. Using this
approach, we can see ourselves as part of a larger
flow of giving and receiving throughout time.
Receiving from the past, we can give to the future.
When tackling issues such as climate change, the
stance of gratitude is a refreshing alternative to
guilt or fear as a source of motivation."
- **Joanna Macy & Chris Johnstone**

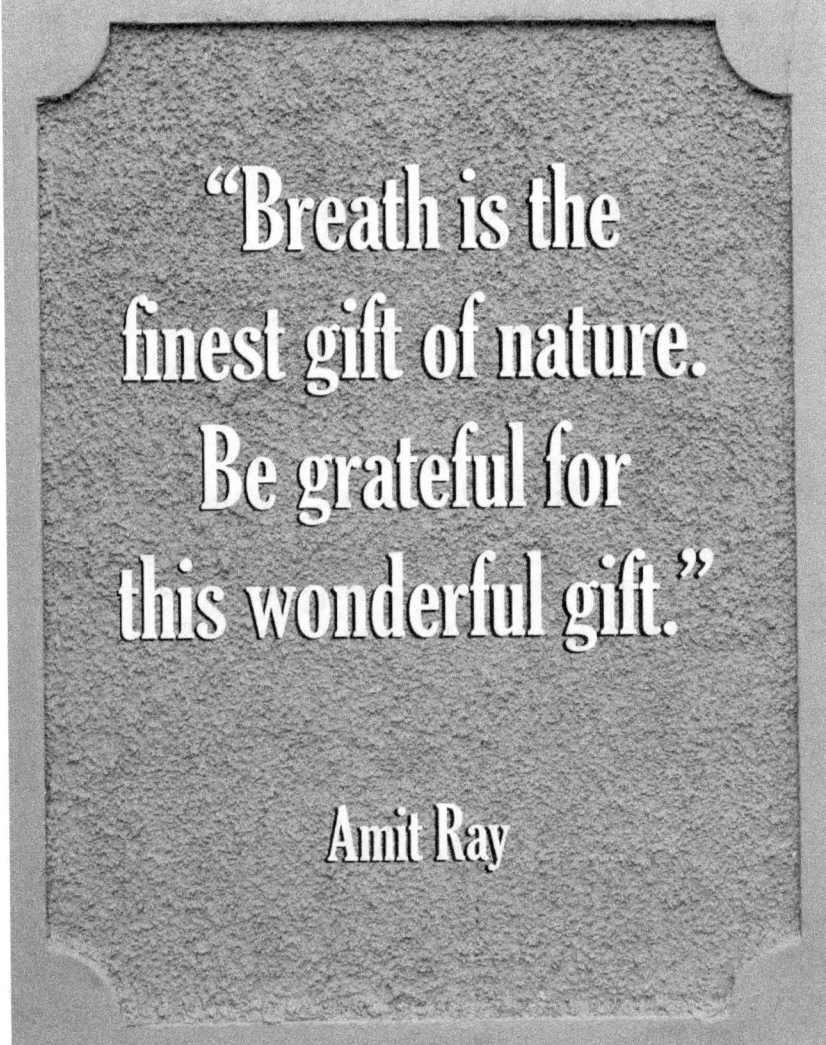

"Thoughts turn to other's just a little more this time of year. Days grow shorter and memories grow longer. Families and friends gather in celebration or hope. Giving is a reflection of our love and caring for each other and those less fortunate. May your thoughts turn to gratitude this holiday season and carry on throughout the next year…"
- James A. Murphy

"When we give cheerfully and accept gratefully, everyone is blessed."
- Maya Angelou

"To have peace in our life we must honour our every moment. Imagine living a full, meaningful and joyous life. Imagine miracles happening all around us. Imagine being filled with awe and gratitude each day, and laying down to sleep each night feeling peaceful and relaxed. We can, if we honour the sacred present in us and around us. Thus we make our lives collectively precious. Every moment is sacred! Being mindful of the sacredness of time encourages us and nurtures our awareness. By honouring every moment, even the 'meaningless' ones, we make them sacred."
- Angie Karan

"Ironically, we may discover that death meditation is not a morbid exercise at all. Only when we lose the use of something taken for granted (whether the telephone or an eye) are we jolted into a recognition of its value. When the phone is fixed, the bandage removed from the eye, we briefly rejoice in their restoration but swiftly forget them again. In taking them for granted, we cease to be conscious of them. In taking life for granted, we likewise fail to notice it. (To the extent that we get bored and long for something exciting to happen.) By meditating on death, we paradoxically become conscious of life."
- Stephen Batchelor

"There are some people who walk into your life and shed a new light in your entire being.
Be grateful to such people."
- Ogwo David Emenike

"With an attitude of gratitude, you can't go wrong. You are already putting it out there into the universe that you are ready to receive more. This is the universal truth. Be thankful for what you have. Your life is already abundant."
- Karen A. Baquiran

"I see the glass half full and
thank God for what I have."
- Ana Monnar

"When my father-in-law, Jan Vuijst, a Dutch
Reformed minister, was on his deathbed, I had a
deeply intimate conversation with him - as it turned
out, my last conversation with him. He said to me, 'It
was a privilege to have lived.' The soulful gratitude
of that simple statement will never leave me."
- Daniel Klein

"Gratitude is a powerful catalyst for happiness. It's
the spark that lights a fire of joy in your soul."
- Amy Collette

"Take full account of what Excellencies you possess,
and in gratitude remember how you would hanker
after them, if you had them not."
- Marcus Aurelius

"Nothing's more gratifying than to get
a heart-felt 'Thank you'!"
- Saurabh Singal

"Feeling gratitude and not expressing it is like
wrapping a present and not giving it."
- William Arthur Ward

"Most of us forget to take time for wonder, praise and gratitude until it is almost too late. Gratitude is a many-colored quality, reaching in all directions. It goes out for small things and for large;
it is a God-ward going."
- Faith Baldwin

"My heart's gratitude is my life's plenitude."
- Sri Chinmoy

"I truly believe we can either see the connections, celebrate them, and express gratitude for our blessings, or we can see life as a string of coincidences that have no meaning or connection. For me, I'm going to believe in miracles, celebrate life, rejoice in the views of eternity and hope my choices will create a positive ripple effect in the
lives of others. This is my choice."
- Mike Ericksen

"An ancient cornerstone of prayer is that our desire to thank God is itself God's gift. Be grateful."
- Richard Leonard

"Appreciating what I have is my medicine."
- Betty Jamie Chung

"Gratitude is a powerful catalyst for happiness. It's the spark that lights a fire of joy in your soul."

Amy Collette

"Focus on your daily blessings, future opportunities and possibilities, and never allow your challenges, struggles, and obstacles to interfere with your peace of mind. You owe abundant happiness and success to your inner-self."
- Edmond Mbiaka

"Gratitude is an antidote to negative emotions, a neutralizer of envy, hostility, worry, and irritation. It is savoring; it is not taking things for granted; it is present oriented."
- Sonja Lyubomirsky

"We can never bring anything to us unless we are grateful for what we have. In fact, if somebody were completely and utterly grateful for everything, they would never have to ask for anything, because it would be given to them before they even asked."
- Rhonda Byrne

"You were formed inside a borrowed womb-a nourishing safe haven for months-then delivered through painful effort and sacrifice by a woman willing to give you the precious gift of life. That truth alone deserves your gratitude and respect."
- Richelle E. Goodrich

"If the only prayer you said was thank you,
that would be enough."
- Meister Eckhart

"Gratitude is not something idyllic that comes when
all good things line up to be counted. Gratitude is
there all the time waiting to be focused on."
- Antonia Montoya

"Pause your opinions, debating and absolute
knowing for long enough to conceive gratitude."
- Bryant McGill

"Find things to be grateful for. It is easy.
You're alive; that's a good thing to start
being grateful for right away."
- Allan G. Hunter

"Thankfulness is the beginning of gratitude.
Gratitude is the completion of thankfulness.
Thankfulness may consist merely of words.
Gratitude is shown in acts."
- Henri Frederic Amiel

"Good Seeds! Gratitude is the Greatest Attitude
that has no Substitute."
- Bernard Kelvin Clive

"If you learn to develop an abundant mentality you will not be envious of others, you will celebrate their successes, you share in their joys and pains; don't see life as a competition but a complimentary."
- Bernard Kelvin Clive

"We have so much for what to be grateful and if we thank for it, we will have even much more."
- Victoria Vorel

"Each moment of gratitude awareness reveals the total beauty which surrounds you."
- Bryant McGill

"The more we express thanks, the more gratitude we feel. The more gratitude we feel, the more we express thanks. It's circular, and it leads to a happier life."
- Steve Goodier

"One grateful thought is a ray of sunshine. A hundred such thoughts paint a sunrise. A thousand will rival the glaring sky at noonday - for gratitude is light against the darkness."
- Richelle E. Goodrich

"Gratitude is born in hearts that
take time to count up past mercies."
- Charles E. Jefferson

"People always complain that they can't do this
and they can't do that."
- Nick Vujicic

"What are you grateful for? Get in the habit of being
grateful, even for a small thing. It opens up your
energy for positivity and blessings to flow to you."
- Eileen Anglin

"The only people with whom you should try to get
even are those who have helped you."
- John E. Southard

"Far better it seems to me, in our vulnerability, is to
look death in the eye and to be grateful every day for
the brief but magnificent opportunity that life
provides."
– Carl Sagan

"Thanksgiving creates abundance."
- Ann Voskamp

"I want to cultivate a deep sense of gratitude, of groundedness, of enough, even while I'm longing for something more. The longing and the gratitude, both. I'm practicing believing that God knows more than I know, that he sees what I can't, that he's weaving a future I can't even imagine from where I sit this morning."
- **Shauna Niequist**

"One can never pay in gratitude; one can only pay 'in kind' somewhere else in life."
- **Anne Morrow Lindbergh**

"When the gratitude that many owe to one discards all modesty, then there is fame."
- **Friedrich Nietzsche**

"I'm grateful for today. I'm stronger, braver, wiser."
- **Tony Curl**

"Living in love, gratitude and forgiveness, is peaceful and spiritually rejuvenating. Living under the emotional constraints of anger and resentment is draining and toxic to heart and soul. It can be difficult to let go of past hurts, but it can also be freeing and uplifting. More and more, i choose to live in love, gratitude and forgiveness."
- **Jaeda DeWalt**

"Ungrateful people forget what they are not grateful for."

Ana Monnar

"Happy are those who value what they have,
when they have it."
- Tammy Rosenfeld

"Remember, whatever you focus upon, increases. . . .
When you focus on the things you need, you'll find
those needs increasing. If you concentrate your
thoughts on what you don't have, you will soon be
concentrating on other things that you had forgotten
you don't have-and feel worse! If you set your mind
on loss, you are more likely to lose. But a grateful
perspective brings happiness and
abundance into a person's life."
- Andy Andrews

"Gratitude always comes into play; research shows
that people are happier if they are grateful for the
positive things in their lives, rather than worrying
about what might be missing."
- Dan Buettner

"I live by three simple words: compassion, love and
gratitude. We need to act on these three words daily.
Doing so will irrevocably change your world."
- Julian Pencilliah

"Gratitude is not just a word; it is a way a of life."
- **Rob Martin**

"What is the one thing that gets you up every morning? The one thing that keeps you going every day, every month, every year? Let me get you started. My one thing is this, 'I'm one day closer...' One day closer to a goal, an outcome, or the results I'm after in my life. This is my way of remembering the importance of focusing on the life I desire and living a life of gratitude! So, what's your one thing...?"
- **James A. Murphy**

"On the road to success, there is always room to share appreciation and gratitude for other people's successes. Feeling gratitude for other people raises our own vibration, while adding cement to the bricks we lay. Finding the best qualities in others allows us to build those qualities within ourselves. And when we focus on our personal growth with open hearts and minds, the speed with which we construct dramatically increases, because all the while, we are attracting more like energy and like-minded people into our lives to assist us."
- **Alaric Hutchinson**

"Love, forgiveness, modesty, humility and gratitude
are most important virtues in life."
- **P. Remes**

"I feel a very unusual sensation - if it is not
indigestion, I think it must be gratitude."
- **Benjamin Disraeli**

"By talking to yourself every hour of the day, you
can direct yourself to think thoughts of courage and
happiness, thoughts of power and peace. By talking
to yourself about the things you have to be grateful
for, you can fill your mind with thoughts
that soar and sing."
- **Dale Carnegie**

"Though they only take a second to say, 'thank you's'
leave a warm feeling behind that can last for hours."
- **Kent Allan Rees**

"Gratitude is medicine for a heart devastated by
tragedy. If you can only be thankful
for the blue sky, then do so."
- **Richelle E. Goodrich**

"'When you are grateful,' Brother Steindl-Rast explained, 'You are not fearful, and when you are not fearful, you are not violent. When you are grateful, you act out of a sense of enough and not out of a sense of scarcity, and you are willing to share. If you are grateful, you are enjoying the differences between people and respectful to all people. The grateful world is a world of joyful people. Grateful people are joyful people. A grateful world is a happy world.'"
- Douglas Carlton Abrams

"Life can be awful. Life can be ugly. And still there are those who smile at the darkness, anticipating the beauty of an eventual sunrise."
- Richelle E. Goodrich

"The miracle is not to walk on water. The miracle is to walk on the green earth, dwelling deeply in the present moment and feeling truly alive."
- Thich Nhat Hanh

"Summoning gratitude is a sure way to get our life back on track. Opening our eyes to affirm gratitude grows the garden of our inner abundance, just as standing close to a fire eventually warms our heart."
- Alexandra Katehakis

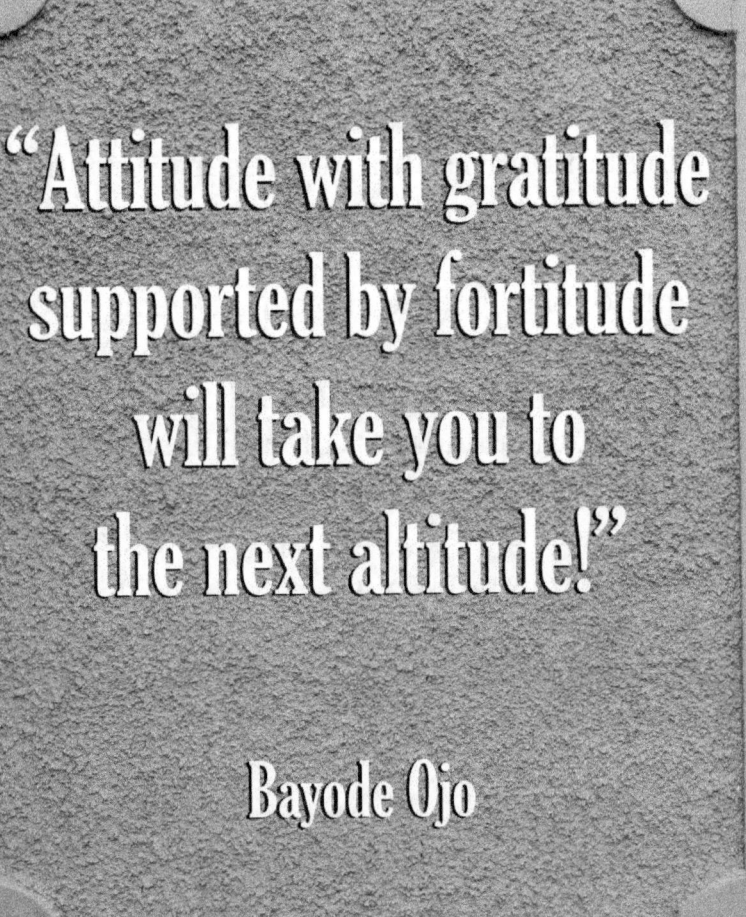

"The Story of Your Life: The world and everyone you meet will not revolve around you. You're not always going to get what you want. You are going to make compromises every single day. You're going to get smacked down a time or two, or three, or fifty. Throwing tantrums, sitting in the corner pouting and crying over what you didn't get that you wanted isn't going to help you get it. Likewise, pissing and moaning to other people about it all being so unfair. We're all in the same boat, my friends. You can choose to sit in the corner and sulk your life away, crying about the unfairness of it all, bemoaning how everyone is making you miserable, or you can do just the opposite. You can stand up and be grateful for everything you do have. You can look back and see how many obstacles you've already overcome, realizing that with each conquest you've become a stronger person. You can realize that your happiness is not and should never be dependent on other people. None of us is going to get out of this story alive, dear reader. Make the best of the time you have. Make a positive difference. Make your own happily ever after."
- **Pamela Morris**

"What is the path to wholeness? We will see this path more clearly if we recognize that greed's ugly stepsister is ungratefulness. Greed always wants more. When we are greedy, we are never satisfied. Whatever we receive from others, we conclude we deserve. And in whatever quantity it may come, it is never enough. Lack of gratitude is a manifestation of an abundance of greed. From the vantage point of the taker, it is his or her justification for always demanding. He is endlessly disappointed in others. No one ever comes through for him. No one ever keeps his promises. Everyone always falls short of his expectations. There is no need for thanks, except thanks for nothing. No truth, no matter how profound, will find its way into a heart that is absent of gratitude."
- Erwin Raphael McManus

"The secret to happiness is complaining very little."
- Nikki Rowe

"With heavy rainfall, the river will overflow its banks. This is spirit of gratitude; the more grateful you are, the more your life overflow with abundance."
- Lailah Gifty Akita

"Feeling grateful or appreciative of someone or something in your life actually attracts more of the things that you appreciate and value into your life."
- Christiane Northrup

"He is a wise man who does not grieve for the things which he has not, but rejoices for those which he has."
- Epictetus

"Gratitude is the experience of our true self."
- Gina Lakes

"Acknowledging the good that you already have in your life is the foundation for all abundance."
- Eckhart Tolle

"Life is a web of intersections and choices. Your 1st choice is to recognize an intersection. Your 2nd choice is to be grateful for it."
- Ryan Lilly

"Gratitude always comes into play; research shows that people are happier if they are grateful for the positive things in their lives, rather than worrying about what might be missing."
- Dan Buettner

"If a fellow isn't thankful for what he's got, he isn't likely to be thankful for what he's going to get."
- **Frank A. Clark**

"Gratitude is nutrition for a living relationship."
- **Steve Maraboli**

"Be thankful for your allotment in an imperfect world. Though better circumstances can be imagined, far worse are nearer misses than you probably care to realize."
- **Richelle E. Goodrich**

"With grace and gratitude, great lives evolve."
- **Lailah Gifty Akita**

"If I only looked at what I've lost, I'd never be able to see what I have."
- **Cindy Charlton**

"In the end, though, maybe we must all give up trying to pay back the people in this world who sustain our lives. In the end, maybe it's wiser to surrender before the miraculous scope of human generosity and to just keep saying thank you, forever and sincerely, for as long as we have voices."
- **Elizabeth Gilbert**

"'Be grateful for the things you don't have that you don't want.'
-Bob Dylan's Dad"

Bob Dylan

"Piglet noticed that even though he had a
Very Small Heart, it could hold a
rather large amount of gratitude."
- A.A. Milne

"With full appreciation, count your blessings no
matter how small they might seem. Gratitude and
unconditional self-love are the best gifts that you
could ever give to your inner-self."
- Edmond Mbiaka

"If you aren't happy for what you already have then
what makes you think you will be happy with more."
- Maddy Malhotra

"For me, every hour is grace. And I feel gratitude
in my heart each time I can meet someone
and look at his or her smile."
- Elie Wiesel

"Happiness cannot be traveled to, owned, earned,
worn or consumed. Happiness is the spiritual
experience of living every minute with
love, grace and gratitude."
- Denis Waitley

"Start each day with a positive thought
and a grateful heart."
- Roy T. Bennett

"Gratitude looks to the Past and love to the Present;
fear, avarice, lust, and ambition looks ahead."
- C.S. Lewis

"In ordinary life, we hardly realize that we receive
a great deal more than we give, and that it is only
with gratitude that life becomes rich."
- Dietrich Bonhoeffer

"When it comes to giving thanks to God, there isn't a
card, a sentiment, a picture, or a word that can
adequately express the gratitude in my heart. What
can I say to the One who not only saved my life but
who also adopted me into His family? How can I
possibly express my thankfulness for His riches?
How can I express my gratitude for His friendship
and His healing touch? How does one find the words
to thank Him for His unconditional love, unmerited
favour, and forgiveness? Dictionaries and
thesauruses can't help me. All I can say is 'Thank
you, God' with the hope that those humble words
convey all that is in my heart."
- Katherine J. Walden

"Appreciation is a wonderful thing. It makes what is excellent in others belong to us as well."
- Voltaire

"Gratitude should run through our veins, it should reside in us, it should live in our bones as long we live."
- Euginia Herlihy

"If we never experience the chill of a dark winter, it is very unlikely that we will ever cherish the warmth of a bright summer's day. Nothing stimulates our appetite for the simple joys of life more than the starvation caused by sadness or desperation. In order to complete our amazing life journey successfully, it is vital that we turn each and every dark tear into a pearl of wisdom, and find the blessing in every curse."
- Anthon St. Maarten

"Ingratitude to God does not rely only on our refusal to give the verbal thanksgiving due to Him, but also recides in our inability to appreciate his gifts and potentials in us by leaving them untapped."
- Israelmore Ayivor

"Gratitude doesn't change the scenery.
It merely washes clean the glass you look through
so you can clearly see the colors."
- Richelle E. Goodrich

"In life one has a choice to take one of two paths:
to wait for some special day -
or to celebrate each special day."
- Rasheed Ogunlaru

"Life's true gift is the capacity to enjoy enjoyment."
– Lwaxana Troi, Star Trek: The Next Generation

"Build your home in small moments of joy,
and you will always feel at home."
- Charlotte Eriksson

"My father had had to explain to me that giving
thanks is not a common practice in India. 'Then how
do you know if people appreciated what you did?'
I'd asked.'Do you really need to know?'
my father had asked back."
- Chitra Banerjee Divakaruni

"I have learned that in every circumstance that comes my way, I can choose to respond in one of two ways: I can whine or I can worship! And I can't worship without giving thanks. It just isn't possible. When we choose the pathway of worship and giving thanks, especially in the midst of difficult circumstances, there is a fragrance, a radiance, that issues forth out of our lives to bless the Lord and others."
- Nancy Leigh DeMoss

"Begin each day with a promise to self to be grateful, be kind, be authentic your day will meet your intent."
- Bluenscottish

"... and isn't the world a treasure in itself? A spectacle glittering every single day, without a concern if anyone's watching or not. It simply goes on, elegantly, letting nature have its way. We only need to open our eyes to witness the biggest masterpiece ever created, the ticket is already in your hand."
- Charlotte Eriksson

"Sincere, heartfelt appreciation is pure love, and is the strongest message to the Universe that this is more of what you want to experience. Feel grateful and attract more reason to be grateful for. It works like magic."
- Malti Bhojwani

"Each moment
of gratitude awareness
reveals the total beauty
which surrounds you."

Bryant McGill

"There is a wave of gratefulness because people are becoming aware how important this is and how this can change our world. It can change our world in immensely important ways, because if you're grateful, you're not fearful, and if you're not fearful, you're not violent. If you're grateful, you act out of a sense of enough and not of a sense of scarcity, and you are willing to share. If you are grateful, you are enjoying the differences between people, and you are respectful to everybody, and that changes this power pyramid under which we live."
- David Steindl-Rast

"The future depends on attitude, aptitude, and gratitude-not on knowledge."
- Debasish Mridha

"I don't have to chase extraordinary moments to find happiness - it's right in front of me if I'm paying attention and practicing gratitude."
- Brené Brown

"Belittling nostalgia is a frightened man's parlor trick. Be grateful for any prize. Even a paper fortress, albeit briefly, provides shelter from the rain."
- Amy Koppelman

"When you express gratitude for the blessings that come into your life, it not only encourages the universe to send you more, it also sees to it that those blessings remain." - Stephen Richards
"And a man can't afford to waste all the good part, worrying about the bad parts. That makes it all bad."
- Fred Gipson

"To evade arrogance, remind yourself (from time to time) that your talent or success could have been better. To be thankful, remind yourself (every now and then) that your illness or failure could have been worse."
- Mokokoma Mokhonoana

"The wonder of life is heart of gratitude."
- Lailah Gifty Akita

"Everything you have ever done has led up to this very moment. Savor your life, the lessons, the wisdom, the failures, the victories and all the relationships that have made an imprint in your journey."
- Karen A. Baquiran

"No duty is more urgent than that of returning thanks".
- Unknown

"To have attracted readers is the most magical part of my writing life. I was not expecting you to show up when I wrote my first books. It took me by surprise. It filled me with gratitude. It still does."
- Pat Conroy

"The happiest people on earth are not those who have robust bank accounts, or all the good things in this world; but, they are those who truly embrace the attitude of gratitude. Some of these folks are poor, but are still very grateful for the little they have; for the peace of mind they enjoy, for the love in their lives, for the unity in their family and for all the ordinary things many people take for granted. They always focused, not on the things they are aspiring for, but for all the things God has used to bless their lives."
- Sesan Kareem

"This a wonderful day. I've never seen this one before."
- Maya Angelou

"Express gratitude for love, joy, and beauty of life, to expand your happiness."
- Debasish Mridha

"Love, positivity and gratitude are the most essential ingredients to a happy and fulfilled life."
- Eileen Anglin

"Be happy, noble heart, be blessed for all the good thou hast done and wilt do hereafter, and let my gratitude remain in obscurity like your good deeds."
- Alexandre Dumas

"Prayers, likewise your positive thoughts, can be based on gratitude and love."
- Raphael Zernoff

"Sometimes I live so much in my mind that I forget what is right before my eyes."
- Anna Quindlen

"Blessed are those that can give without remembering and receive without forgetting."
– James Allen Proctor

"Gratitude turns what we have into enough, and more. It turns denial into acceptance, chaos into order, confusion into clarity...it makes sense of our past, brings peace for today, and creates a vision for tomorrow."
- Melody Beattie

"The more
you appreciate,
the more you have
to appreciate."

Carma Spence

"The truest indication of gratitude is
to return what you are grateful for."
- Richard Paul Evans

"Life-changing gratitude does not
fasten to a life unless nailed through
with one very specific nail at a time."
- Ann Voskamp

"Gratitude of heart can often
be seen in a generous spirit."
– Our Daily Bread Devotions

"Be thankful for the efforts of people who worked
hard to get you where you are; you should not take it
for granted and treat them with indifference."
- Roy T. Bennett

"Gratitude is a harbinger of healing,
the first robin of spring."
- Joyce Wycoff

"A purpose is more like a positive daily-grind,
with gratitude and a smile."
- Bryant McGill

"You can't be passionate about gratitude and
be crippled by ingratitude."
- Bamigboye Olurotimi

"We often take for granted the very things that
most deserve our gratitude."
- Cynthia Ozick

"Amazement + Gratitude + Openness + Appreciation
= an irresistible field of energy"
- Frederick Dodson

"Gratitude is a divine shift in your perspective from
one of separation and lack to one of unity and right
mindedness. It is a choice not made from guilt but
rather from a higher level of consciousness."
- Janet Rebhan

"My relationship with him was defined by these
complex emotions, this mixture of gratitude and
resentment."
– Otsuichi

"Never let them try out this gratitude, for they would
immediately discover that it supplies the first and
most important component to happiness:
Contentment."
- Geoffrey Wood

"Find the light. Reach for it. Live for it.
Pull yourself up by it. Gratitude always
makes for straighter, taller trees."
- **Al R. Young**

"Give thanks for a little and you will find a lot."
- **The Hausa of Nigeria**

"As you lay yourself down to sleep tonight, think of
something you are grateful for. Bless someone who
was kind to you, and forgive someone who wasn't."
- **Eileen Anglin**

"The deepest craving of human nature is
the need to be appreciated."
- **William James**

"In ordinary life we hardly realize that we receive a
great deal more than we give, and that it is only with
gratitude that life becomes rich."
- **Dietrich Bonhoeffer**

"Steam seems to have killed all gratitude
in the hearts of sailors."
- **Jules Verne**

"Attitude with gratitude supported by fortitude will take you to the next altitude!"
- Bayode Ojo

"If you have true gratitude, it will express itself automatically. It will be visible in your eyes, around your being, in your aura. It is like the fragrance of a flower. In most cases if there is a beautiful flower, the fragrance will be there naturally. The flower and its fragrance cannot be separated."
- Sri Chinmoy

"The grateful heart sits at a continuous feast."
- Proverbs 15:15

"I truly believe we can either see the connections, celebrate them, and express gratitude for our blessings, or we can see life as a string of coincidences that have no meaning or connection. "Live everyday like your birthday and drive your life with all varieties of appreciation. A life live with thanksgiving every day is never tired of being lived again and again!"
- Israelmore Ayivor

"If a fellow isn't thankful for what he's got, he isn't likely to be thankful for what he's going to get."
- Frank A. Clark

"Be grateful for whatever it is that opens you up."
- Allan G. Hunter

"I can only see life as this most miserable accident that I have been forced to endure simply because I refuse to see it as the most astounding plan that I have been privileged to engage."
- Craig D. Lounsbrough

"The only people who you should get even with are those who have helped you."
- John Southard

"Even discomfort or pain delivers awareness of life, and an opportunity for gratitude."
- Bryant McGill

"If the heights of our joy are measured by the depths of our gratitude, and gratitude is but a way of seeing, a spiritual perspective of smallness might offer a vital way of seeing especially conducive to gratitude."
- Ann Voskamp

"Once we forget those who have contributed time and effort in making an endeavor successful, we forget ourselves."
- Beem Weeks

"You have the power
to adjust
your life experience
simply by
being grateful."

Chiara Gizzi

"Gratitude and attitude are not challenges;
they are choices."
- **Robert Braathe**

"Each day brings new opportunities, allowing you to
constantly live with love-be there for others-bring a
little light into someone's day. Be grateful
and live each day to the fullest."
- **Roy T. Bennett**

"By simple mathematics giving is key to the world
you seek to live in. If I take I alone gain. If I give or
share then two at least are enriched."
- **Rasheed Ogunlaru**

"When we maintain a conscious connection
with Gratitude, our presence will naturally
radiate a certain beauty and undisturbed,
inner tranquility. Such individuals glow.
All such individuals look beautiful and seem
irresistible to those who value goodness. They
have an attractor field of loveliness which, likewise,
tends to bring out the beauty in other people."
- **Donna Goddard**

"Whatever you appreciate and give thanks for
will increase in your life."
- **Sanaya Roman**

"A sense of entitlement is a cancerous thought process that is void of gratitude and can be deadly to our relationships."
- Steve Maraboli

"Being grateful does not mean that everything is necessarily good. It just means that you can accept it as a gift."
- Roy T. Bennett

"The reason that so many fail to find happiness is that they fail to find gratitude."
- Rasheed Ogunlaru

"A basic law: the more you practice the art of thankfulness, the more you have to be thankful for."
- Norman Vincent Peale

"More Miracles occur from Gratitude and Forgiveness than anything else"
- Philip H. Friedman

"Now and then it's good to pause in our pursuit of happiness and just be happy."
- Guillaume Apollinaire

"You simply will not be the same person two months from now after consciously giving thanks each day for the abundance that exists in your life. And you will have set in motion an ancient spiritual law: the more you have and are grateful for, the more will be given you"
- Sarah Ban Breathnack

"The attitude of gratitude gives you the right rectitude and sound attitude towards life"
- Sesan Kareem

"Some people grumble that roses have thorns; I am grateful that thorns have roses."
- Alphonse Karr

"Be grateful for what you already have while you pursue your goals. If you aren't grateful for what you already have, what makes you think you would be happy with more."
- Roy T. Bennett

"Give and receive with gratitude. Do the former, without expectation of, the latter."
- Jaeda DeWalt

"Every day of life is a gift! Be sure to... unwrap it.
Play with it. And, most importantly,
give thanks for it!"
- Valerie Rickel

"Gratitude is a way of creativity."
- Nadia Bandura

"Gratitude is the memory of the heart."
– Massieu

"The problem with the world, is, far too many
people drain their energy into what is wrong
with their life; instead of holding gratitude
for what's right in their life."
- Nikki Rowe

"When we saw a destitute-looking man trying to sell
worn flip-flops, I vowed never to complain about a
job again. When I considered the steady paycheck
and quality of life it provided, my past gripes -
primarily boring meetings, back-biting office politics
and pantyhose - were just whining."
- Kristine K. Stevens

"If I only looked
at what I've lost,
I'd never be able
to see
what I have."

Cindy Charlton

"Let gratitude be the pillow upon which you kneel to say your nightly prayer. And let faith be the bridge you build to overcome evil and welcome good."
- **Maya Angelou**

"Gratitude takes less energy than anger."
- **Kristin Cashore**

"My expectations were reduced to zero when I was 21. Everything since then has been a bonus."
- **Stephen Hawking**

"Ungrateful people forget what they are not grateful for."
- **Ana Monnar**

"Gratitude leads to a good attitude"
- **Habeeb Akande**

"Expectation has brought me disappointment. Disappointment has brought me wisdom. Acceptance, gratitude and appreciation have brought me joy and fulfilment."
- **Rasheed Ogunlaru**

"The good news is that being in gratitude
does not require time and money. All it requires
is an attitude of being grateful."
- Vishwas Chavan

"At times, our own light goes out and is rekindled
by a spark from another person. Each of us has cause
to think with deep gratitude of those who
have lighted the flame within us."
- Albert Schweitzer

"Life is difficult for us all. We're all driven by love,
and the desire to be loved and happy. If you take the
right attitude, you think positively, you fill yourself
with gratitude, joy and passion – it could be hell
on earth and you'd still be happy."
- K.A. Hill

"The value we place on what we've been given
correlates to our depth of gratitude for it."
- Todd Stocker

"Can you be grateful for everything?
No. But in every moment."
- David Steindl-Rast

"If you are reading this, be sure to count this on your blessings list."
- **Anthony Liccione**

"The best antidote to the furtive poison of anger, fear, anxiety, or any of our destructive, unwieldy passions, is just gratitude. And not the grandiose, boisterous or especially obvious kind. It is not necessarily the verbose or expressive kind. It's often the full immersion, a kind of deep submersion even, into a pool of awareness. This penitent affect distills within us surreal realizations; it is a focus, tinged with layers of deep remorse and the profound beauty of newfound appreciation that washes over us about the simplest things we have slipped into, or suddenly become aware of our own complacency over. This cooling antidote instantly soothes any veins swollen with the heat of pride, or stopped up with pearls of finely polished self-pity. This all comes about with a balm of humility that is simultaneously soothing and jolting to all of our senses at the same time. It is a cocktail both sedative and stimulant in the same, finite instant. It often occurs as we are halted dead in our tracks by a thing so extraordinary and breathtakingly natural, even luscious in its simplicity and unusually ordinary existence; often something we have been blatantly negligent of noticing as we routinely trudge past it in our self-absorbed haze."
- **Connie Kerbs**

"Because gratitude is the key to happiness, anything that undermines gratitude must undermine happiness. And nothing undermines gratitude as much as expectations. There is an inverse relationship between expectations and gratitude: The more expectations you have, the less gratitude you will have."
- Dennis Prager

"Rather than getting more spoilt with age, as difficulties pile up, epiphanies of gratitude abound."
- Alain de Botton

"I am fortunate to be a resemblance, rather than a replication of who I was yesterday."
- Rob Martin

"You have the power to adjust your life experience simply by being grateful."
- Chiara Gizzi

"Happiness begins with gratitude."
- Dr. MaryAnn Diorio

"Nothing is so fundamental to the spiritual life
as learning to give thanks."
- **Gordon T. Smith**

"Even just taking 20 seconds to truly appreciate your
surroundings makes a world of difference."
- **Russell Eric Dobda**

"We only live once. We all have an expiration date
after that we will never come again. I am not saying
that to make you sad. I am saying that so you can
cherish each moment in your life and be grateful that
you are here and you are Special"
- **Pablo**

"Nightmare and dream both are not real, but I do
always love my nightmare; because it offers me
gratitude while the latter makes me disappointed."
- **M.F. Moonzajer**

"The shortest road man walks,
is sadly the road of gratitude!"
- **Avra Amar Filion**

"A generous heart filled with gratitude is a magnet for abundance."

Debasish Mridha

"This morning I woke up before the alarm clock went off and the sky outside was a big red ocean. You're beautiful when you're sleeping so I spent an hour observing the way you breathe. Inhale, exhale, without a thought of tomorrow. The window was open and the air was so crisp and I couldn't imagine how to ever ask for more than this."
- **Charlotte Eriksson**

"When you arise in the morning, give thanks for the morning light, for your life and strength. Give thanks for your food and the joy of living. If you see no reason for giving thanks, the fault lies with yourself."
- **Tecumseh**

"Courtesies of a small and trivial character are the ones which strike deepest in the grateful and appreciating heart."
- **Henry Clay**

"I want to remember to notice the wonders of each day, in each moment, no matter where I am under any circumstance."
- **Charlotte Eriksson**

"When you focus on gratitude, positive things flow in more readily, making you even more grateful."
- Lissa Rankin

"If you're not grateful for what you already have, why should you be blessed with more..."
- Germany Kent

"Gratitude is the bridge that merges your love with longevity. It is the vital ingredient for a lasting relationship."
- Steve Maraboli

"Silent gratitude isn't very much to anyone."
- Gertrude Stein

"Entitlement is such a cancer, because it is void of gratitude."
- Adam Smith

"Today you will envy the blessings of another, or you will bask in the wonder of the amazing grace you have been given."
- Paul David Tripp

"There is a law of gratitude, and it is . . . the natural principle that action and reaction are always equal and in opposite directions. The grateful outreaching of your mind in thankful praise to supreme intelligence is a liberation or expenditure of force. It cannot fail to reach that to which it is addressed, and the reaction is an instantaneous movement toward you."
- Wally Wattles

"Service and gratitude will fuel your relationship; entitlement and expectation will poison it."
- Steve Maraboli

"While the ingrates duke-it-out about the true God, you take each breath in holy gratitude."
- Bryant McGill

"Even the smallest blessing on earth is enough reason to be thankful for your life."
- Edmond Mbiaka

"Nothing that is done for you is a matter of course. Everything originates in a will for the good, which is directed at you. Train yourself never to put off the word or action for the expression of gratitude."
- Albert Schweitzer

"When your heart aligns with the truth of its energy, gratitude sings your name, love flows freely, and every bit of your being is awakened, breathing and moving in perfect harmony."
- Angie Karan

"To live, to truly live, one must consider each and every thing a blessing."
- Kamand Kojouri

"Gratitude is what you feel. Thanksgiving is what you do."
- Tim Keller

"We all feel better when we are grateful. There is great wisdom in understanding that no matter the situation, there is always something for which we can choose to be grateful."
- Andy Andrews

"The best way to achieve great success is to learn from wise people. Use them extensively with love, gratitude, and humility."
- Debasish Mridha

"You glorify God with gratitude."
- Corey M.K. Hughes

"Acknowledging the good that you already have in your life is the foundation for all abundance."

Eckhart Tolle

"I am grateful for hands to tickle with. Not so grateful for that process in reverse, however."
- **Richelle E. Goodrich**

"It has been said that life has treated me harshly; and sometimes I have complained in my heart because many pleasures of human experience have been withheld from me...if much has been denied me, much, very much, has been given me..."
- **Helen Keller**

"Thank you, Tempest, for loving me when understanding was too hard. Thank you for understanding when loving me is impossible."
- **Tracy Deebs**

"You should always be thankful and express gratitude for your love, beauty, family, and everything in your life."
- **Debasish Mridha**

"Thank God I was hit by a truck. It seems that God was trying to get my attention for years but I was so stubborn it took knocking me square out of my body to see him for myself. Next time I will be way more specific when I ask for help to slow me down."
- **Monika Zands**

"Gratitude, like faith, is a muscle. The more you use
it, the stronger it grows, and the more power you
have to use it on your behalf. If you do not practice
gratefulness, its benefaction will go unnoticed, and
your capacity to draw on its gifts will be diminished.
To be grateful is to find blessings in everything.
This is the most powerful attitude to adopt,
for there are blessings in everything."
- Alan Cohen

"I will one day accept death with gratitude if I meet it
having lived a life that became truly my own."
- Dan Pearce

"Feeling entitled is the opposite of feeling grateful.
Gratitude opens the heart, entitlement closes it."
- Paul Gibbons

"It's better to find success through God,
than finding it on one's own merits; some who
usually find their own success become boastful,
where through God it's with gratitude."
- Anthony Liccione

"Gratitude comes in a spectrum of colors,
but Ingratitude is always black."
- Ankala V. Subbarao

"True happiness is to enjoy the present, without anxious dependence upon the future, not to amuse ourselves with either hopes or fears but to rest satisfied with what we have, which is sufficient, for he that is so wants nothing. The greatest blessings of mankind are within us and within our reach. A wise man is content with his lot, whatever it may be, without wishing for what he has not."
- Seneca

"Don't count your blessings,
let your blessings count! EnjoyLife!"
- Bernard Kelvin Clive

"If you are really thankful,
what do you do? You share."
- W. Clement Stone

"Great things happen to those who don't stop believing, trying, learning, and being grateful."
- Roy T. Bennett

"By acknowledging spirit with gratitude, you bring it joy and give it more strength to do its work."
- Russell Eric Dobda

"Living in constant love and gratitude
is the essence of spirituality."
- **Akemi G**

"Gratitude is an overflow of
the pleasure filling your soul."
- **Raheel Farooq**

"Gratitude goes beyond the 'mine' and 'thine' and
claims the truth that all of life is a pure gift. In the
past I always thought of gratitude as a spontaneous
response to the awareness of gifts received, but now I
realize that gratitude can also be lived as a discipline.
The discipline of gratitude is the explicit effort to
acknowledge that all I am and have is given to me as
a gift of love, a gift to be celebrated with joy."
- **Henri J.M. Nouwen**

"You must understand that it is not in the nature of
Man to be grateful. So, in whatever you or I do for
others we must never expect gratitude. If we do,
we will only be disappointed."
- **S.R. Nathan**

"To improve quality of life, to evolve into a better version of ourselves, to pause in recognition of blessings with only our name on the tag, to dance in graitutde, to embrance with abandon, to give without receiving, to seek the face of God ... all this and more is why we exisit."
- **Toni Sorenson**

"... this counting blessings was the unlocking of the mystery of joy, joy, 'the gigantic secret of the Christian,' joy hiding in gratitude ... God had used the dare to give me this; led me all the way to give me this, live fully, fully live."
- **Ann Voskamp**

"Life is a whirlwind of many opportunities. Choose to embrace all of them in deepest gratitude. Learn to forgive yourself and honour the heart that beats within you, as well as the head that rests on your shoulders. Learn how to believe in people again and not be judging or cynical to various beliefs."
- **Michelle Cruz-Rosado**

"Only a stomach that rarely feels hungry scorns common things."
– **Horace**

"Love, positivity and gratitude are the most essential ingredients to a happy and fulfilled life."

Eileen Anglin

"I am awake, I see the sun. I am going to give my gratitude to the sun and to everything and everyone because I am still alive. One more day to be myself."
- Miguel Ruiz

"Disappointment, fear, grief, unlove, dullness and guilt are the worst feelings. Learn from them so that you move on. Then replace them with more satisfying and promising joy, love gratitude, pride, confidence, direction."
- Diana Jaber

"Appreciate the things and people in your life while remaining independent of them. Give thanks for them, but realize that they do not complete you. Only you can complete you."
- Serenity Rey

"The more you are grateful for what you have the more you can live fully in the present. When you live in the present moment the greater you can build stepping stones for a brighter future."
- Dana Arcuri

"Joy is the simplest form of gratitude."
- Karl Barth

"Hurry always empties a soul."
- Ann Voskamp

"I was holding the door for several girls in front of you, and I waited for you to catch up. When you reached me, you looked pleased, and a little surprised. Unlike the others, you didn't expect the door to be held for you by some random guy. You smiled up at me and said, 'Thank you."
- Tammara Webber

"Gratitude makes you a better, stronger, wiser person. Ingratitude makes you a negative, angry, miserable person.
Which person do you choose to be?"
- Tanya Masse

"It isn't what you have in your pocket that makes you thankful, but what you have in your heart."
-James Allen Proctor

"Gratitude enables you to be fearless, and to never shy away from reveling in every moment of your life."
- Janice Anderson

"Every day, tell at least one person something you
like, admire, or appreciate about them."
- **Richard Carlson**

"Life is beautiful if you see it
with the eyes of gratitude."
- **Qasim Chauhan**

"I have learned over a period of time to be almost
unconsciously grateful-as a child is-for a sunny day,
blue water, flowers in a vase, a tree turning red. I
have learned to be glad at dawn and when the sky is
dark. Only children and a few spiritually evolved
people are born to feel gratitude as naturally as they
breathe, without even thinking. Most of us come
to it step by painful step, to discover that gratitude
is a form of acceptance."
- **Faith Baldwin**

"Road accidents, psycho killings, plane crashes
abound - we don't know which day will be our last,
so why not make today the happiest day and be
thankful for all that we have?"
- **Maddy Malhotra**

"Gratitude is a soul blooming profusely!"
- **Zavia Hope Thomas**

"When you open to your heart, your entire world changes-it opens up around you. You see yourself as part of a friendly universe, one that is full of possibility, one that is generating and regenerating a positive energy."
- Baptist de Pape

"Amidst all the bacchanal and confusion in your life, find something to be grateful for, even if it is the air that you breath and trust me, this will transform you in some small way. Gratitude is really the great multiplier."
- Akosua Dardaine Edwards

"'Enough' is a feast.
- Buddhist proverb

"Carpe Diem... I express my gratitude for everything in my life. What else is possible?"
- Ron Barrow

"Today, I don't want to ask for anything. I just want to give thanks for everything I already have."
- Nikki Rowe

"If a fellow isn't thankful for what he's got, he isn't likely to be thankful for what he's going to get."

Frank A. Clark

"Learning to appreciate the beauty that surrounds you is one of the keys to your happiness."
- Tom Giaquinto

"When you start with thanksgiving, you will always end with praise. Be thankful, it grows."
- TemitOpe Ibrahim

"As each day comes to us refreshed and anew, so does my gratitude renew itself daily. The breaking of the sun over the horizon is my grateful heart dawning upon a blessed world."
- Adabella Radici

"Be happy for things that work."
- Na'ama Yehuda

"The more we thank God, the less we ask of him."
- Ron Brackin

"Make enthusiasm a way of life. Make optimism a way of success. Make gratitude a way of happiness."
- Debasish Mridha

"Keep a gratitude list."
- Steve Maraboli

"By and large, people who are grateful, happy
and enthusiastic are going to demonstrate better
performance than those who are unhappy
and unappreciative. There is increasing evidence
that a grateful mindset amplifies happiness
and mental and emotional wellbeing."
- Christopher Dines

"Every day is a gift and a very special day; so let us
celebrate with joy and profound gratitude."
- Debasish Mridha

"We owe some of our successes to people
who did not want to help us more than we do
to those who have helped us."
- Mokokoma Mokhonoana

"Pity is not forgiveness, nor is gratitude absolution."
- Pierce Brown

"Gratitude is the heart's first language."
- Joey Garcia

"My creed is this: To make sure that every single ounce of true kindness given to me, will never be forgotten, and not only remain unforgotten, but that those acts of true kindness will multiply and bear fruit just because they were planted in me. To make people's acts of true kindness towards me multiply like investments. That's my creed. So that a person who has bestowed a goodness upon me, will never be able to regret that act and will in fact say to herself or himself 'I am so glad that I did that for her, it's one of the best things I've ever done. A good investment.' And I know for sure that the people who have shown me any amount of true kindness, can say for certain, that it's one of the best things they've done in life, because I make sure that they can say that about me. Ask anyone who's been kind to me, and they will tell you. Because this is my creed in life. There is no greater evil, in my opinion, than the evil that infests a person who takes for granted any amount of true kindness given to her/him. To forget a kindness done unto you, is to be just like a donkey. Donkeys might even be better. And so this is the creed that I live by."
- C. JoyBell C.

"Life-giving ministry flows from lives that are full of gratitude to God, not with an expectation of gratitude from others."
- Christopher L. Heuertz

"Humility, gratitude, and generosity – three things you can never go wrong with."
- **Kevin J. Donaldson**

"Say thank you for a beautiful life and be grateful for the small things of life which are miracles we have actually got used to. Gratitude banishes negativity from your life, brings happiness and you start living in abundance and attract more love and prosperity because of the way you think about your life."
- **Sanchita Pandey**

"The world concerns me only in so far as I owe it a certain debt and duty, so to speak, because I have walked this earth for 30 years, and out of gratitude would like to leave some memento in the form of drawings and paintings-not made to please this school or that, but to express a genuine human feeling."
- **Vincent Van Gogh**

"Every once in a while, God allows you to stub your toe as a kind reminder to be grateful for the miraculous body attached to it."
- **Richelle E. Goodrich**

"To speak gratitude is courteous and pleasant, to enact gratitude is generous and noble, but to live gratitude is to touch Heaven."
- Johannes A. Gaertner

"In life, as in knitting, don't leave loose ends. Take the time to thank the people who matter in your life."
- Reba Linker

"Beware: It is a quick transition from a nourishing sense of gratitude to a poisonous sense of entitlement."
- Steve Maraboli

"Gratitude is unquestionably one of the major keys to attracting more blessings and living a quality life."
- Edmond Mbiaka

"Beth ceased to fear him from that moment, and sat there talking to him as cozily as if she had known him all her life, for love casts out fear, and gratitude can conquer pride."
- Louisa May Alcott

"Be thankful for what you have. Be thankful for what you wish you have. Be thankful for what you are capable of having."
- Lailah Gifty Akita

"Want what you have,
and then you can
have what you want."

Frederick Dodson

"Gratitude unlocks the door of opportunities, blessing, greatness and prosperity. Gratitude is your key to a worthy life."
- **Sesan Kareem**

"When we accept ourselves for what we are, we decrease our hunger for power or the acceptance of others because our self-intimacy reinforces our inner sense of security. We are no longer preoccupied with being powerful or popular. We no longer fear criticism because we accept the reality of our human limitations. Once integrated, we are less often plagued with the desire to please others because simply being true to ourselves brings lasting peace. We are grateful for life and we deeply appreciate and love ourselves."
- **Brennan Manning**

"Whenever we are appreciative, we are filled with a sense of well-being and swept up by the feeling of joy."
- **M.J. Ryan**

"Reflect upon your present blessings, of which every man has plenty; not on your past misfortunes, of which all men have some."
- **Charles Dickens**

"The way to develop the best that is in a person is by appreciation and encouragement."
- Charles Schwab

"Your attitude of gratitude will bring you altitude in business and multitude in blessings."
- Farshad Asl

"Gratitude is a way of life.
Gratitude is the way home."
- Angie Karan

"Gratitude and attitude are not challenges; they are choices."
- Robert J. Braathe

"Practice appreciation for who you are and what you have… and allow your life to unfold in the most amazing way."
- Millen Livis

"Walking in shoes bigger than your feet, will inspire gravity to pull you down. Let's be grateful for what fits us...for what we have."
- Dr. Jacinta Mpalyenkana

"Without darkness, we may never know how bright the stars shine. Without battles, we could not know what victory feels like. Without adversity, we may never appreciate the abundance in our lives. Be thankful, not only for the easy times, but for every experience that has made you who you are."
- Julie-Anne

"Even the smallest tender mercy can bring peace when recognized and appreciated."
- Richelle E. Goodrich

"The more I understand the mind and the human experience, the more I begin to suspect there is no such thing as unhappiness; there is only ungratefulness."
- Steve Maraboli

"Thanksgiving is not only being aware of the abundance of good in the world but embracing it."
- Richelle E. Goodrich

"It is impossible to feel grateful and depressed in the same moment."
- Naomi Williams

"If we all counted our blessings and then shared
them with our neighbors, near and far,
all our lives would be richer."
- Janet Autherine

"Here is the world, and you live in it, and are
grateful. You try to be grateful."
- Michael Cunningham

"When I started counting my blessings,
my whole life turned around."
- Willie Nelson

"Our receiving expands with our gratitude."
- Bryant McGill

"Contentment and gratitude are signs that
you are worthy of further receivership."
- Bryant McGill

"Gratitude is more of a compliment
to yourself than someone else."
- Raheel Farooq

"Making the ungrateful grateful
is a tedious endeavor."
- Ana Monnar

"Now and then
it's good to pause
in our pursuit
of happiness
and just be happy."

Guillaume Apollinaire

"He is a wise man who does not grieve for
the things which he has not, but rejoices for
those which he has."
- Epictetus

"Many people who order their lives rightly in all
other ways are kept in poverty
by their lack of gratitude."
- Wallace Wattles

"Whatever our individual troubles and challenges
may be, it's important to pause every now and then
to appreciate all that we have, on every level. We
need to literally "count our blessings," give thanks
for them, allow ourselves to enjoy them, and relish
the experience of prosperity we already have."
- Shakti Gawain

"If we do not feel grateful for what we already have,
what makes us think we would be
happy with more?"
- John A. Passaro

"Be grateful for the day and the day will be grateful
for you. Stay positive and everything around you
will respond in kind."
- TemitOpe Ibrahim

"Some people can be so generous
when they give nothing away!"
- Rossana Condoleo

"Gratitude is the key to manifestation, for gratitude
connects you directly to the source."
- Abhishek Kumar

"Be thankful for everything that happens in your life;
it's all an experience."
- Roy T. Bennett

"Give thanks to the earth for the hospitality and
generosity; Show gratitude for life, light
and every little beauty."
- Debasish Mridha

"The things that people were the most grateful for
were the ordinary things in life. The sound of your
spouse's laugh, the smell of morning coffee, the echo
of children playing in the yard. The little things. In
waiting for the big moments-the vacations, the
retirements, the birthdays-we risk missing the
experiences of life most worthy of celebrating."
- John O'Leary

"[One} who does not know when a gift has made him safe is poorer than a slug, even though he may think otherwise himself."
- Richard Adams

"If we look at our lives and concentrate on things that we don't have or wish to have, that doesn't change the circumstances. The truth is that we have to focus on what we have and make the best out of it."
- Nick Vujicic

"Both abundance and lack exist simultaneously in our lives, as parallel realities. It is always our conscious choice which secret garden we will tend... when we choose not to focus on what is missing from our lives but are grateful for the abundance that's present - love, health, family, friends, work, the joys of nature and personal pursuits that bring us pleasure - the wasteland of illusion falls away and we experience Heaven on earth."
–Sarah Ban Breathnach

"With all respect to your religion or world-view - thank God, thank the universe, thank evolutionary processes - the keyword is "thank" - just have some gratitude and be thankful."
- Bryant McGill

"True wisdom is being able to say 'it is what it is' with a smile of celebratory wonder on your face."
- Eric Micha'el Leventhal

"When it comes to life the critical thing is whether you take things for granted or take them with gratitude."
- G.K. Chesterton

"He thought about his long life and gave thanks for all the bounty and joy that he had been given. To want more, to wish for yet more, he knew, would be petty. He sighed happily, and listened to the wind sweeping down from the mountains, to the chirping of night birds."
- Khaled Hosseini

"You say, 'If I had a little more, I should be very satisfied.' You make a mistake. If you are not content with what you have, you would not be satisfied if it were doubled." - Charles Haddon Spurgeon
"In the past I always thought of gratitude as a spontaneous response to the awareness of gifts received, but now I realize that gratitude can also be lived as a discipline. The discipline of gratitude is the explicit effort to acknowledge that all I am and all I have is given to me as a gift of love, a gift to be celebrated with joy."
- Henri Nouwen

"Gratitude for the seemingly insignificant-a seed-this plants the giant miracle."
- **Ann Voskamp**

"Gratitude helps you to grow and expand; gratitude brings joy and laughter into your life and into the lives of all those around you."
- **Eileen Caddy**

"Grateful people are happy people. The more things you are grateful for, the happier you will be."
- **Roy T. Bennett**

"Keep your eyes open and try to catch people in your company doing something right, then praise them for it."
- **Tom Hopkins**

"Gratitude is more of a compliment to yourself than someone else."
- **Raheel Farooq**

"Those who have the ability to be grateful are the ones who have the ability to achieve greatness."
- **Steve Maraboli**

"Find magic in
the little things,
and the big things
you always expected
will start to show up."

Isa Zapata

"How would your life be different if...you began
each day by thanking someone who has helped you?
Let today be the day...You make it a point to show
your gratitude to others. Send a letter or card, make
a call, send a text or email, tell them in person...
do whatever you have to do to let them
know you appreciate them."
- Steve Maraboli

"Being able to appreciate who we are and
what we have in the now is an easy way to
journey through this life."
- Raphael Zernoff

"Regardless of sunshine or rain, be thankful
for another great day...and treat life as
the ultimate gift.... because it is :)"
- Pablo

"Let's start with what we can be thankful for,
and get our mind into that vibration, and then
watch the good that starts to come, because
one thought leads to another thought."
- Bob Proctor

"In the Christian community thankfulness is just what it is anywhere else in the Christian life. Only he who gives thanks for little things receives the big things. We prevent God from giving us the great spiritual gifts He has in store for us, because we do not give thanks for daily gifts. We think we dare not be satisfied with the small measure of spiritual knowledge, experience, and love that has been given to us, and that we must constantly be looking forward eagerly for the highest good. Then we deplore the fact that we lack the deep certainty, the strong faith, and the rich experience that God has given to others, and we consider this lament to be pious. We pray for the big things and forget to give thanks for the ordinary, small (and yet really not small) gifts. How can God entrust great things to one who will not thankfully receive from Him the little things? If we do not give thanks daily for the Christian fellowship in which we have been placed, even where there is no great experience, no discoverable riches, but much weakness, small faith, and difficulty; if on the contrary, we only keep complaining to God that everything is so paltry and petty, so far from what we expected, then we hinder God from letting our fellowship grow according to the measure and riches which are there for us all in Jesus Christ."
- Dietrich Bonhoeffer

"Don't wait to celebrate life until you retire, because you never know the day you will expire."
- Maddy Malhotra

"Appreciate your mom. She is wiser than you think and stronger than you know. Be thankful."
- Steve Maraboli

"Your life looks like a prison because you focus on the things you wish you had and thus don't appreciate what you already have. So why don't you try to see the abundance in your life? Because, if you haven't noticed, you've got many things to thank for. Just look around."
- Lidiya K.

"Gratitude is a currency that we can mint for ourselves, and spend without fear of bankruptcy."
- Fred De Witt Van Amburgh

"To have more, you must genuinely thank more."
- Maddy Malhotra

"'Keep an attitude of gratitude!' gratitude is the key to manifestation, for gratitude connects you directly to the source."
- Abhishek Kumar

"The things that most deserve our gratitude we just take for granted. Without air we cannot live for more than a minute or two. Everyday we are breathing in and breathing out, but do we ever feel grateful to the air? If we do not drink water, we cannot survive. Even our body is composed to a large extent of water.But do we give any value to water? Every morning when we open our eyes, we see the sun blessingfully offering us light and life-energy, which we badly need. But are we grateful to the sun?"
- Sri Chinmoy

"To receive, you must be active. Keep in mind your purpose. You will receive in direct proportion to your clarity of vision, your definiteness of purpose, the steadiness of your faith, and the depth of your gratitude."
- John-Roger

"Gratitude is riches. Complaint is poverty."
- Doris Day

"To give thanks in solitude is enough. Thanksgiving has wings and goes where it must go. Your prayer knows much more about it than you do."
- Victor Hugo

"Gratitude
bestows reverence
...changing forever
how we experience
life and the world."

John Milton

"Happiness isn't complicated. It is a humble state of gratitude for simple pleasures, tender mercies, recognized blessings, and inherent beauty."
- Richelle E. Goodrich

"We can be thankful to a friend for a few acres or a little money; and yet for the freedom and command of the whole earth, and for the great benefits of our being, our life, health, and reason, we look upon ourselves as under no obligation."
- Marcus Annaeus Seneca

"When you arise in the morning, think of what a precious privilege it is to be alive-to breathe, to think, to enjoy, to love-then make that day count!"
- Steve Maraboli

"I think I run my strongest when I run with joy, with gratitude, with focus, with grace."
- Kristin Armstrong

"When you become addict in to material things in life, then the true natural life starts to run away from you. Yes! it can give you certain pleasure in the society, but in the same time it will sabotage your true happiness of life which we could have simply with gratitude and forgiveness"
- Rashedur Ryan Rahman

"You live one time on earth.
Live each day with thankful heart."
- Lailah Gifty Akita

"Love, gratitude, compassion, and kindness are
the sources of all enduring, pure happiness."
- Debasish Mridha

"What I've learned is there's a scientifically proven
phenomenon that's attached to gratitude, and that if
you consciously take note of what is good in your
life, quantifiable benefits happen."
- Deborah Norville

"When I intentionally thank God for the good gifts
that come from being his child, I find it almost
impossible to maintain my sour disposition."
- Lori Hatcher

"Keep your head up and heart open. And make
'Thank You' your mantra of life!"
- Abhishek Kumar

"My gratitude to him is as boundless
as the Pacific Ocean."
- Yann Martel

"You cannot define success and do that exceptionally well without a mention of 'gratitude'."
- Unarine Ramaru

"Love of God is pure when joy and suffering inspire an equal degree of gratitude."
- Simone Weil

"There is, however, a far more common ailment among us-and that is pride from the bottom looking up. It is manifest in so many ways, such as faultfinding, gossiping, backbiting, and murmuring, living beyond our means, envying, coveting, withholding gratitude and praise that might lift another, and being unforgiving and jealous."
- Ezra Taft Benson

"A dog is grateful for what is, which I am finding to be the soundest kind of wisdom and very good theology."
- Carrie Newcomer

"When you thank God for what you have, it means you appreciate and value what's in your hands. And when you value what's in your hands, it will open up its wonder to you."
- TemitOpe Ibrahim

"The most beautiful moments in life are moments when you are expressing your joy, not when you are seeking it."
- Sadhguru

"Gratitude isn't a tool to manipulate the universe or God. It's a way to acknowledge our faith that everything happens for a reason even if we don't know what that reason is.
-Melody Beattie

"In life, one has a choice to take one of two paths: to wait for some special day or to celebrate each special day."
- Rasheed Ogunlaru

"Cultivating an attitude of gratitude begins with counting your blessings. In simpler terms, gratitude is expressing thanks for gifts we receive. Genuine gratitude helps us to see the little things in life that are often overlooked, yet so precious."
- Dana Arcuri

"Gratitude is one of the greatest Christian virtues; ingratitude, one of the most vicious sins."
- Billy Graham

"Gratitude is where every positive attitude starts."
- **Michael Hyatt**

"Being grateful is the bridge between the world of nightmares and the world where we are free to say no. It's the bridge between the world of delusions and the world of creativity. It's the power that brings death back to life, the power that turns poverty to wealth and anger to compassion."
- **James Altucher**

"Gratitude is the best food and fuel to start the day for you. Have some at lunchtime and again at dinner too. It will energise and sustain you - the whole day through. But it will also leave you room, power and the thirst to do what you need to do and contribute."
- **Rasheed Ogunlaru**

"Gratitude becomes spiritual, a spiritual virtue and a spiritual emotion, when we are moved in our response by a God-centered view of the three: gift, recipient, and giver."
- **Ray A.**

"Ingratitude is a crime more despicable than revenge, which is only returning evil for evil, while ingratitude returns evil for good."
- **William George Jordan**

"Things turn out best
for people who
make the best of the
way things turn out."

John Wooden

"If you concentrate on finding whatever is
good in every situation, you will discover that
your life will suddenly be filled with gratitude,
a feeling that nurtures the soul."
- Harold Kushner

"Having contentment and gratitude in the present
moment is the surest way to achieve success."
- Bryant McGill

"He was fortified by a memory which kept only
the good things and rejected the ill. Despite
his sorrows, he had had a fair share of joys
and these were ever fresh and accessible."
- Evelyn Waugh

"He who does not reflect his life back to God
in gratitude does not know himself."
- Albert Schweitzer

"The number one joy indicator, the one thing that
will predict whether someone feels joy in their life or
not, is the practice of gratitude."
- John O'Leary

"As we learn to give thanks for all of life and death,
for all of this given world of ours, we find a deep joy.
It is the joy of trust, the joy of faith in the faithfulness
at the heart of all things. It is the joy of gratefulness in
touch with the fullness of life."
- **David Steindl-Rast**

"If I do not feel a sense of joy in God's creation,
if I forget to offer the world back to God with
thankfulness, I have advanced very little upon
the Way. I have not yet learnt to be truly human.
For it is only through thanksgiving that
I can become myself."
- **Kallistos Ware**

"Always be grateful with the small things
because they are the beginning of
bigger and better things to come."
- **Edmond Mbiaka**

"Gratitude therefore takes nothing for granted,
is never unresponsive, is constantly awakening to
new wonder and to praise of the goodness of God.
For the grateful person knows that God is good,
not by hearsay but by experience. And that
is what makes all the difference."
- **Thomas Merton**

"Life doesn't owe us anything. We only owe ourselves, to make the most of the life we are living, of the time we have left, and to live in gratitude."
- Bronnie Ware

"There is no prescription for finding moments of gratitude in every day; there is simply the choice."
- Gillian Deacon

"Got no checkbooks, got no banks. Still I'd like to express my thanks - I've got the sun in the mornin' and the moon at night."
- Irving Berlin

"[I] never talk about gratitude and joy separately, for this reason. In 12 years, I've never interviewed a single person who would describe their lives as joyful, who would describe themselves as joyous, who was not actively practicing gratitude."
- Brené Brown

"It's amazing how the more thankful I am, the more things I get to be thankful for."
- Jeanette Coron

"Be attached to nothing. Be grateful for everything."
- David Che

"Dance. Smile. Giggle. Marvel. Trust. Hope.
Love. Wish. Believe. Most of all, enjoy
every moment of the journey, and
appreciate where you are at this moment instead
of always focusing on how far you have to go."
- Mandy Hale

"Most humbling of all is to comprehend the
lifesaving gift that your pit crew of people has been
for you, and all the experiences you have shared, the
journeys together, the collaborations, births and
deaths, divorces, rehab, and vacations, the solidarity
you have shown one another. Every so often you
realize that without all of them, your life would be
barren and pathetic. It would be Death of a Salesman,
though with e-mail and texting."
- Anne Lamott

"Gratitude is an excellent attitude which can lift you
to a greater altitude if you put it on as a vesture."
- S. E. Entsua-Mensah

"In the modern world we are surrounded by, so
much abundance that we cannot see it."
- Chris Matakas

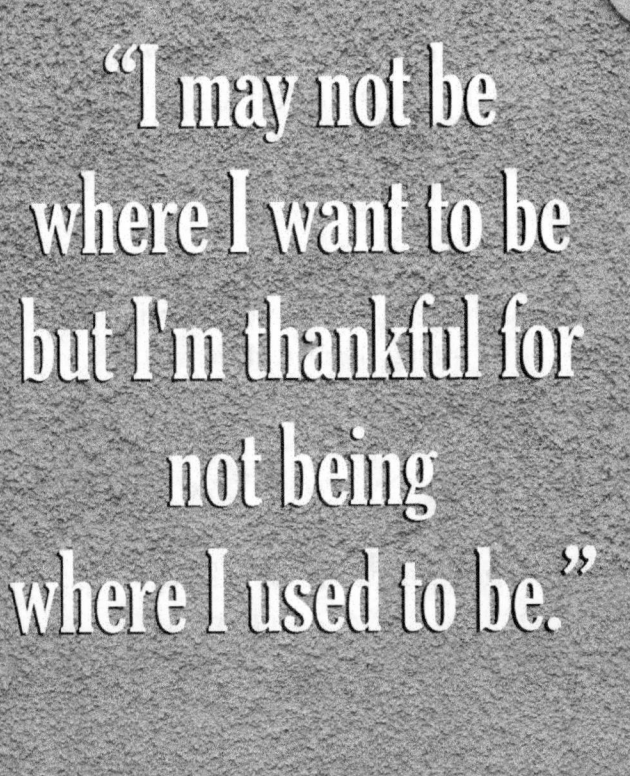

"I may not be
where I want to be
but I'm thankful for
not being
where I used to be."

Joyce Meyer

"Gratitude unlocks the fullness of life. It turns what we have into enough, and more. It turns denial into acceptance, chaos to order, confusion to clarity. It can turn a meal into a feast, a house into a home, a stranger into a friend. Gratitude makes sense of our past, brings peace for today and creates a vision for tomorrow."
- Melody Beattie

"Of course gratitude should be expressed...But that does not mean to kill your self-esteem."
- Deepika Muthusamy

"I believe we can choose Love and gratitude, or choose Other Than. Those are our options, and in the end, there's only one option."
- Kelly Corbet

"Every New Year is the same. Every day, every second is too for that matter. But when we deliver them in secret, when another year just begins as a matter of fact, it's easy to fail to appreciate what a miracle it is to have more time. So, I suppose, it feels different right now because this time you're paying attention"
- Hillary DePiano

"Gratitude is not only the greatest of virtues,
but the parent of all others."
- Marcus Tullius Cicero

"Let us never be afraid of innocent joy; God is good
and what he does is well done; resign yourself to
everything, even happiness; ask for the spirit of
sacrifice, of detachment, of renunciation, and above
all, for the spirit of joy and gratitude."
– Henri-Frédéric Amiel

"You can also look at your body and think about how
the blood flows and the fact that your body is in
constant renewal. It is a miracle of creation
happening within you every second of the day.
This is something to be thankful for."
- Celso Cukierkorn

"The word "Eucharist" means literally "act of
thanksgiving." To celebrate the Eucharist and to live
a Eucharistic life has everything to do with gratitude.
Living Eucharistically is living life as a gift, a gift for
which one is grateful. But gratitude is not the most
obvious response to life, certainly not when we
experience life as a series of losses! Still, the great
mystery we celebrate in the Eucharist and live in a
Eucharistic life is precisely that through mourning
our losses we come to know life as a gift."
- Henri J.M. Nouwen

"Begin with thanking Him for some little thing, and then go on, day by day, adding to your subjects of praise; thus you will find their numbers grow wonderfully; and, in the same proportion, will your subjects of murmuring and complaining diminish, until you see in everything some cause for thanksgiving. If you cannot begin with anything positive, begin with something negative. If your whole lot seems only filled with causes for discontent, at any rate there is some trial that has not been appointed you; and you may thank God for its being withheld from you. It is certain that the more you try to praise, the more you will see how your path and your lying down are beset with mercies, and that the God of love is ever watching to do you good."
- Priscilla Maurice

"Your ability to see beauty and possibility is proportionate to the level at which you embrace gratitude."
- Steve Maraboli

"Gratitude builds a bridge to abundance."
- Roy Bennett

"Those who are not grateful soon begin to complain of everything."
- Thomas Merton

"Sometimes, we wait on God for special things to happen extraordinarily in our lives before we understand that "God is working". Meanwhile, there are "super-special" things that fill our life barrels in minute drops, but they go unappreciated!"
- **Israelmore Ayivor**

"Let us be grateful to the people who make us happy; they are the charming gardeners who make our souls blossom."
- **Marcel Proust**

"Not immediately able to proceed, I stood there, inexpressibly grateful that my life, for all its terrors, is so filled with moments of grace."
- **Dean Koontz**

"You must appreciate beauty for it to endure."
- **Pat Conroy**

"I am not interested in having the world revolve around me; that's too boring of an idea. I would rather revolve around the world and try to leave my fingerprints, everywhere. My fingerprints mingled in with all the other fingerprints and all the laughter and all the beautiful things like gratitude, grace, faithfulness and flowers."
- **C. JoyBell C.**

"When we
give cheerfully
and accept gratefully,
everyone is blessed."

Maya Angelou

"Two kinds of gratitude: The sudden kind
we feel for what we take; the larger kind
we feel for what we give."
- Edwin Arlington Robinson

"The world has enough beautiful mountains and
meadows, spectacular skies and serene lakes. It has
enough lush forests, flowered fields, and sandy
beaches. It has plenty of stars and the promise of a
new sunrise and sunset every day. What the world
needs more of is people to appreciate and enjoy it."
- Michael Josephson

"It's a privilege to love someone, to truly love them;
and while it's paradisaical if she or he loves you back,
it's unfair to demand or expect reciprocity. We
should consider ourselves lucky, honored, blessed
that we possess the capacity to feel tenderness of
such magnitude and be grateful even when that love
is not returned. Love is the only game in which
we win even when we lose."
- Tom Robbins

"Possession of wealth is not the happiness
but expression of gratitude for the possession
is the happiness."
- Debasish Mridha

"When you lose a beloved belonging, rather than being unkind to yourself, imagine finding it and feeling relief and joy. Sometimes when things get lost, it's a reminder to appreciate all you still have. The experience of reconnecting with something you love and use often increases one's sense of gratitude."
- Laura Staley

"None of those material possessions do anything to make your life any better... I know a lot of people who have a lot of everything, and they're absolutely the most miserable people in the world. So it won't do anything for you unless you're a happy person and can have peace with yourself."
- Lenny Kravitz

"Life, liberty and the pursuit of gratitude, now that would've worked. They would have been readily led to contentment, which would've then better lead them on to happiness."
- Geoffrey Wood

"Never let the things you want make you forget the things you have."
- Sanchita Pandey

"Those who are too arrogant to say thank you find boredom in life. They are often depressed, unhappy and lived an empty life."
- Sesan Kareem

"Take note and give thanks for all the good things present in your life."
- Amey Hegde

I don't need to go to heaven or hell. I have been both places and always wanted more. I will settle for somewhere in between, so eternity never becomes dull and every miracle is something I never take for granted."
- Shannon L. Alder

"Be grateful to those who refuse your demands. They are your benefactors."
- Marty Rubin

"Cultivate the habit of being grateful for every good thing that comes to you, and to give thanks continuously. And because all things have contributed to your advancement, you should include all things in your gratitude."
- Ralph Waldo Emerson

"It turns out that there are many powers of the heart-
among them intuition, intention, gratitude,
forgiveness, resilience, and, of course, love."
- Baptist de Pape

"Gratitude can transform common days into
thanksgivings, turn routine jobs into joy, and change
ordinary opportunities into blessings."
- William Arthur Ward

"Gratitude is the sweetest thing in a seeker's life- in
all human life. If there is gratitude in your heart, then
there will be tremendous sweetness in your eyes."
- Sri Chinmoy

"Ask. Trust. Give thanks. Simple; right?"
- Dawn Gluskin

"Gratitude is an art of painting an adversity
into a lovely picture."
– Kak Sri

"It's easy and natural to be thankful
when your expectations are met. The real test
of your faith is when things don't go your way,
or when you are in pain."
- Maddy Malhotra

"Kindness is as simple as being grateful for the love anyone has shown you, by not destroying them because it isn't on your terms."
- Shannon L. Alder

"Getting lost in the 'big picture' often prevents us from cherishing the 'small moments' that make it all worthwhile..."
- J.R. Wirth

"The best way to pay for a lovely moment is to enjoy it."
- Richard Bach

"True gratitude, not mere verbal platitudes of thanks, is also a power in and of itself, which bursts forth from our inner being to the universe. Having received this power, the universe must respond, allowing more gifts to come our way."
- Stephen Richards

"Gratitude, not guilt, as motivation is always His starting point, thus guilt as a motivation leads nowhere."
- Geoffrey Wood

"If the only prayer
you said was
thank you,
that would
be enough."

Meister Eckhart

"I am grateful for all the trials
for that made be a better person."
- Lailah Gifty Akita

"The most fortunate are those who have a wonderful
capacity to appreciate again and again, freshly and
naively, the basic goods of life, with awe, pleasure,
wonder and even ecstasy."
- Abraham H. Maslow

"Don't over-focus on the negatives and
under-focus the positives in your life."
- Lalah Delia

"God smiles when we praise and thank Him
continually. Few things feel better than receiving
heartfelt praise and appreciation from someone else.
God loves it, too. An amazing thing happens
when we offer praise and thanksgiving to God.
When we give God enjoyment, our own hearts
are filled with joy."
- William Law

"What are you addicted to: being thankful for your
blessings or moaning about your problems?"
- Maddy Malhotra

"Cultivate a thankful spirit! It will be to thee a perpetual feast. There is, or ought to be, with us no such thing as small mercies; all are great, because the least are undeserved. Indeed, a really thankful heart will extract motive for gratitude from everything, making the most even of scanty blessings."
- John Ross Macduff

"I thought I had nothing to be grateful for today, but then the universe became quiet a moment so I could hear my heart beat to the rhythm of my life."
- Karen A. Baquiran

"Always watch your attitude, never forget to express your gratitude."
- Debasish Mridha

"The soul that gives thanks can find comfort in everything; the soul that complains can find comfort in nothing."
- Hannah Whitall Smith

"When eating bamboo sprouts, remember the man who planted them."
- Chinese Proverb

"... most of my prayers are expressions of sheer gratitude for the fullness of my contentment."
- **Elizabeth Gilbert**

"The more emphasis we put on wanting things to change, the more unpeaceful we will be. The more emphasis we put on accepting and having gratitude for 'What is' the closer we are to arriving at Nirvana."
- **Matthew Donnelly**

"Life works with balance. If you give and receive out of giving, you create a balance with life. You serve life, before you expect life to serve you."
- **Roshan Sharma**

"Gratitude opens a clenched fist and a closed heart."
- **Debasish Mridha**

"Gratitude is the antidote for misery. When you are counting your blessings you are too busy to be counting your problems."
- **Miya Yamanouchi**

"All that we have and don't have is a grace. Even the awareness of grace is a grace in which we should give thanks."'
- **Mac MacKenzie**

"What separates privilege from
entitlement is gratitude."
- **Brené Brown**

"We cannot fully heal if we cannot experience
gratitude on a daily basis."
- **Sharon E. Rainey**

"All you need is 5min or even less.....Go outside,
look up the clear sky and thank the heavens above
you for the life you have and the blessings you
receive on a daily basis. Why do we make it a
mission to simply say thank you?"
- **Katlego Semusa**

"The more grateful you are, the more you
attract things to be grateful for."
- **James Altucher**

"Gratitude is the vitamin of the soul."
- **Angie Karan**

"We should live every day like people who have just
been rescued from the moon."
- **Thch Nht Hnh**

"We should certainly count our blessings, but we should also make our blessings count."

Neal A. Maxwell

"Be thankful for your achievements; be thankful for your accomplishments, no matter how big or small. Be thankful for the mind to complete the accomplishments. Be thankful for your past, present, and future. And know that if you are creating success stories you will find that average is how you began, above average is then where you will stand! Lest you forget the strong develop and improve; the weak get frantic, digress and deviate."
- K. Abernathy

"It was possible to love life, without loving your life."
- Christopher Coe

"Have the wisdom to perceive all there is to be thankful for, and then be thankful for the wisdom to perceive things so clearly."
- Richelle E. Goodrich

"Embracing an attitude of gratitude is nourishing to the soul. When we allow ourselves to be engulfed in gratitude, this abundant soul nourishment overflows to your relationships, careers, and day to day lives. Act in gratitude today… If you are grateful to those you love, show them. If you are grateful to those who have helped you, show them. If you are grateful to your creator, to your family, to your friends, and you want it to be known, let it be shown!"
- Steve Maraboli

"Gratitude and love are always multiplied when you give freely. It is an infinite source of contentment and prosperous energy."
- Jim Fargiano

"Once I thought it delightful and astonishing to find a present so big that it only went halfway into the stocking. Now I am delighted and astonished every morning to find a present so big that it takes two stockings to hold it, and then leaves a great deal outside; it is the large and preposterous present of myself."
- G.K. Chesterton

"Thank you, Father, for another day, for another week, for another month and for another year. Your grace is sufficient for me."
- Euginia Herlihy

"In my life, John has been the epitome of gratitude, and not just because he responds to every meal as if it were the best he'd ever eaten. Throughout the many years of our friendship I have learned that John lives on the breath of gratitude and his response is always celebratory. If an exclamation point had arms and legs, its name would be John."
- Mary Morrell

"Work filled with inspiration is worship.
A heart filled with courage is unbreakable.
A life filled with gratitude is fulfilled."
- G.G. Renee Hill

"Not what we say about our blessings, but how we use them, is the true measure of our thanksgiving."
- W.T. Purkiser

"Embrace your journey and those who come across your path. Be gracious in your endeavors. Focus on your craft. Those who support your dreams now and feel your sincere humility and gratitude will be there 20, 30, 40 years from now, padding your old bones and time worn, weary soul."
- Ann Marie Frohoff

"Give Thanks - Get Happy"
- Jane Park Smith

"Thankfulness is the beginning of gratitude.
Gratitude is the completion of thankfulness.
Thankfulness may consist merely of words.
Gratitude is shown in acts."
- Henri-Frédéric Amiel

"The more adept we become at feeling love and gratitude for all life's earthly learning experiences, the more quickly we are reminded that, whatever hardship may be placed before us, it is our choice always to return to a place of love and gratitude and to give thanks for all that still remains."
- Molly Friedenfeld

"If you want to find happiness, find gratitude."
- Steve Maraboli

"Be grateful for everything. The good, the bad, the ugly. Our entire life is a precious gift. It's all part of our path."
- Dawn Gluskin

"An attitude of gratitude brings great things."
- Yogi Bhajan

"Only having valued a thing, can you truly be thankful. You cannot be sincerely thankful for what you have not valued."
- TemitOpe Ibrahim

"Gratitude is pure happiness. Happiness is sure perfection."
- Sri Chinmoy

"Gratitude is the heart of humility, and humility is the path to peace, love, and understanding."
- Justin Young

"For success, positive attitude and gratitude is more important that ability."
- Debasish Mridha

"Always recompense kindness with hearty love and gratitude."
- Debasish Mridha

"Gratitude magnifies the sweet parts of life and diminishes the painful ones."
- Yuval Levin

"Making the ungrateful grateful will bring tears to your eyes, tears of blood bleeding from the heart."
- Ana Monnar

"Gratitude is the ability to experience life as a gift. It liberates us from the prison of self-preoccupation."
- John Ortberg

"Gratitude is where self-love begins!"
- Bryant McGill

"A basic law:
the more you practice
the art of thankfulness,
the more you have
to be thankful for."

Norman Vincent Peale

"The abundance of ordinary things, their convenient
arrangement here, seemed for the moment a personal
gift to me. As did my ability to notice this,
to be grateful for it."
- **Sue Miller**

"When you accept your value and have gratitude,
you are declaring your worthiness of
further receivership."
- **Bryant McGill**

"I always wake up in morning with a big smile
of gratitude on my face. 'Why is that?' Well, every
single day to me is a great opportunity to
push myself closer to the bigger picture
that God has painted for me."
- **Edmond Mbiaka**

"Look at everything as though you were seeing it
for the first or the last time, then your time
on earth will be filled with glory."
- **Betty Smith**

"Start each day with thoughts of gratitude
and you will attract the power of love."
- **Debasish Mridha**

"When we reside in Gratitude, it is impossible to
simultaneously feel like a victim."
- Dr. Theresa Nicassio

"When complimented, a sincere "thank you" is
the only response required."
- H. Jackson Brown Jr.

"There are only two ways to live your life. One is
as though nothing is a miracle. The other is
as though everything is a miracle."
- Albert Einstein

"I am ambitious. I set goals; not because I am
ungrateful for what I have, but because I am happy
with who I am. I enjoy the experience of
rising above my perceived limitations and
discovering new levels of my capabilities."
- Steve Maraboli

"Find the good and praise it."
- Alex Haley

"To increase the value of your day, add some
love and gratitude to your coffee and
some kindness to your dinner."
- Debasish Mridha

"Forget yesterday-it has already forgotten you.
Don't sweat tomorrow-you haven't even met.
Instead, open your eyes and your heart
to a truly precious gift-today."
- Steve Maraboli

"I have come to realize that truly rich people are rich
not because they are frugal or they chose to be frugal,
but because they are so grateful, contented and
full of self-worth that they don't have to prove
anything to anyone with material possessions.
This way, they appear frugal."
- Jan Mckingley Hilado

"Deeply happy people are even thankful for
the trials and tragedies they pass through."
- Auliq-Ice

"We should certainly count our blessings,
but we should also make our blessings count."
- Neal A. Maxwell

"There are three things that stop people from
becoming their best, 'fear' 'anger' and 'greed.' The
antidote to fear is action, the cure for anger is
gratitude and the medicine to greed is love."
- Sesan Kareem

"A mindset of gratitude lifts the veil of bitterness
and allows you to see beauty and possibility."
- Steve Maraboli

"Count your blessings and be grateful
not a great fool."
- Habeeb Akande

"Gratitude opens our eyes to
miracles that surround us. Life's a miracle and a gift.
Take every breath in gratitude"
- D. Denise Dianaty

"Having unceasingly grateful life requires
demonstrating gratitude daily
whether our daily life treats us kindly or not."
- Assegid Habtewold

"An appreciating heart radiates happiness; Gratitude
fills your life with bliss and joyfulness."
- Debasish Mridha

"Like all lawyers, I was delighted by gratitude.
It happened so rarely."
- C.J. Sansom

"Ingratitude produces pride while gratitude produces humility."

Orrin Woodward

"This a a wonderful day.
I've never seen this one before."
- Maya Angelou

"Receiving, gratitude, and generosity
all grow together."
- Mark V. Ewert

"When we become more fully aware that
our success is due in large measure to the loyalty,
helpfulness, and encouragement we have received
from others, our desire grows to pass on similar gifts.
Gratitude spurs us on to prove ourselves worthy
of what others have done for us. The spirit of
gratitude is a powerful energizer."
- Wilferd A. Peterson

"None is more impoverished than the one who
has no gratitude. Gratitude is a currency that
we can mint for ourselves, and spend
without fear of bankruptcy."
- Fred De Witt Van Amburgh

"That sense of entitlement is precisely where
we want them because the right to happiness
is directly opposed to one of The Adversary's
greatest curatives -gratitude."
- Geoffrey Wood

"When you appreciate what you have, and feel
enthusiasm for life, you move in the direction of your
natural state, i.e. happy & peaceful."
- Hina Hashmi

"Family gathers to share good noise and good food.
Gratitude abounds."
- Richelle E. Goodrich

"Clearly, one of the major obstacles to our experience
of gratitude is the habit we have of sleepwalking
through life. The truth is that we are never lacking
for blessings in our lives, but we are often lacking in
awareness and recognition of them."
- Rev. Diane Berke

"Gratitude shifts your focus from what your life lacks
to the abundance that is already present."
– Marelisa Fábrega

"Greed and Lust never say, "Enough!"
- Ron Brackin

"To all of you who have made my being alive so
wonderful, so exciting and so full, my thanks and all
my love."
- Edward Albee

"Open your eyes and see how many gifts there are to unwrap. Notice the presence of your presents. It's not your life that is disappointing: it's your mind."
- **Gregg Krech**

"Gratitude is a form of worship in its own right, as it implies the acceptance of a power greater than yourself."
- **Stephen Richards**

"Aim for happiness because if you keep looking to reach perfection, you're never going to appreciate anything."
- **Karen A. Baquiran**

"When we begin to view our experiences through the lens of gratitude, our heart, mind and spirit naturally expand."
- **David Brown Jr.**

"It is imperative for our mental health that we surround ourselves with like-minded people."
- **Rob Martin**

"We must find time to stop and thank the people who make a difference in our lives."
- **John F. Kennedy**

"Every night before I go to sleep I say out loud three things that I am grateful for, all the significant, insignificant, extraordinary, ordinary stuff of my life. It is a small practice and humble, and yet, I find I sleep better holding what lightens and softens my life ever so briefly at the end of the day."
- Carrie Newcomer

"I find that the more willing I am to be grateful for the small things in life, the bigger stuff just seems to show up from unexpected sources, and I am constantly looking forward to each day with all the surprises that keep coming my way!"
- Louise L. Hay

"I make a point to appreciate all the little things in my life. I go out and smell the air after a good, hard rain. I re-read passages from my favorite books. I hold the little treasures that somebody special gave me. These small actions help remind me that there are so many great, glorious pieces of good in the world."
- Dolly Parton

"Gratitude is heaven itself."
- William Blake

"For every person who closed the door in my face, thank you. For every person who told me I wasn't good enough, thank you. For every person who laughed and told me that I was wasting my time going to college, because I was going to fail, thank you. For every person who tried to break me, thank you. For every person who took my kindness for weakness, thank you. For every person who told me I was wasting time chasing my dreams because I would fail, thank you. It could of broke me. From the core of my heart, I thank you. I truly mean it, because if it weren't for each of you I wouldn't be who I am today. I wouldn't of spend hours and loss sleep studying. I wouldn't developed tough skin. You pushed me to think about what I 'really' want out of life. You pushed me to master my craft. You helped me develop the drive, passion and determination. You pushed me to not wait for someone to believe in my vision, but to find a way to make things happen. I know you didn't "intend" to, but I thank you for teaching me to believe in myself! and you taught me to trust in God and lean on my faith, not man. Thank You!"
- Yvonne Pierre

"Approach the goal you've set with a positive, grateful attitude, and your perception about the goal and the journey will feel less like work, and more like fun."
- John Manning

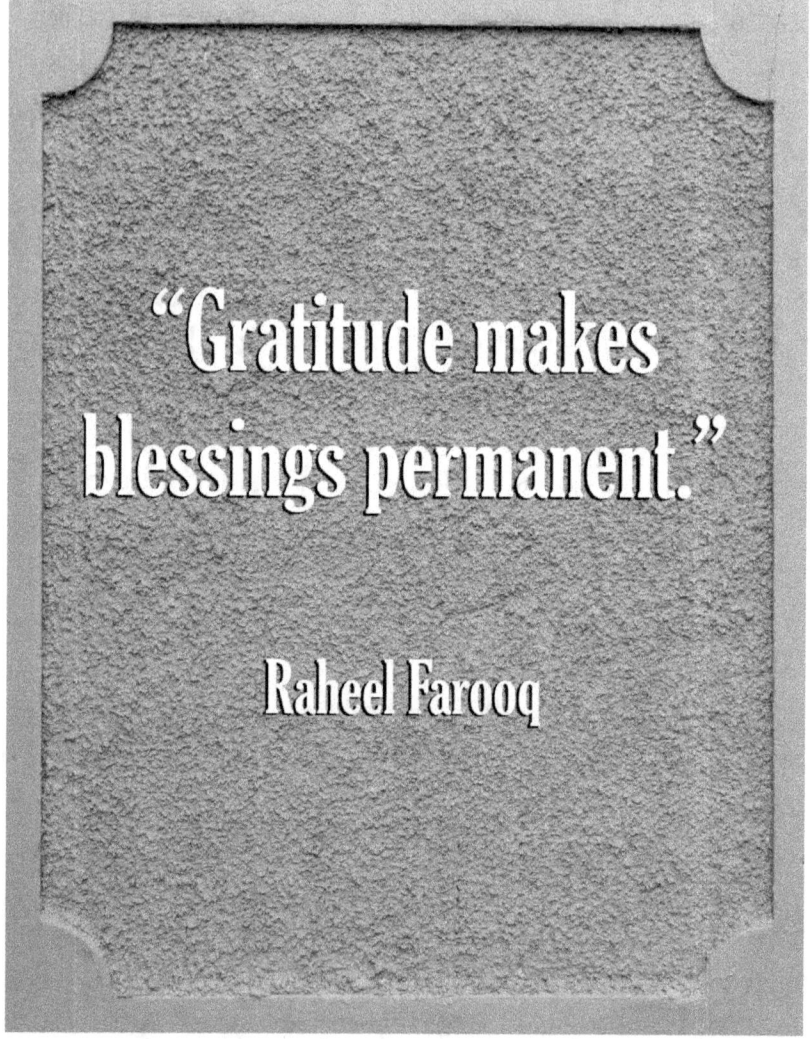

"Holding the space for yourself: Embrace the here and now. Embrace the journey. Try not to judge yourself but rather try to accept yourself as you are. Success is measured in staying on the path, not in how many successes or failures you've had along the way. Let gratitude fill your heart, live with love, laugh and enjoy the journey. All of life is a journey."
- Akiroq Brost

"Every morning and every night, I pause for just a minute and express my gratitude for all that I have in my life and all that I have experienced."
- M. James Airey

"Those who really can receive bread from a stranger and smile in gratitude, can feed many without even realizing it. Those who can sit in silence with their fellow man not knowing what to say but knowing that they should be there, can bring new life in a dying heart. Those who are not afraid to hold a hand in gratitude, to shed tears in grief, and to let a sigh of distress arise straight from the heart, can break through paralyzing boundaries and witness the birth of a new fellowship, the fellowship of the broken."
- Henri J.M. Nouwen

"True forgiveness is when you can say,
'Thank you for that experience.'"
– Oprah Winfrey

"An attitude of gratitude,
is life's most powerful affirmation"
- Angie Karan

"What if you gave someone a gift, and they neglected
to thank you for it-would you be likely to give them
another? Life is the same way. In order to attract
more of the blessings that life has to offer, you must
truly appreciate what you already have."
- Ralph Marston

"Attempt to be creative for the joy it brings . . . select
something like music, dance, sculpture, or poetry.
Being creative will help you enjoy life.
It engenders a spirit of gratitude."
- Richard G. Scott

"Real life isn't always going to be perfect or go our
way, but the recurring acknowledgement of what is
working in our lives can help us not only to survive
but surmount our difficulties."
- Sarah Ban Breathnach

"Gratitude for every day along the way is the key to
acknowledging and enjoying happiness now. Not
when the results come in or when you retire, or when
this or that happens."
- Bronnie Ware

"A sick person is Allah's guest for as long as he is ill. Every day he is sick, God gives him countless rewards, as long as he says 'Alhamdulillah', praise be to God, and does not fight it and complain. When God returns to him his health, he expiates his sins and gives him the status of the newly-born (completely pure and free of any sin). Illness is a mercy and a blessing."
- Kristiane Backer

"To move forward, simply set your intentions, be grateful for what you have, be open to what is possible, and the rest will happen, as a beautiful and effortless journey of cooperation and listening."
- Bryant McGill

"Be grateful for life. Show gratitude to others, whether it's verbally or energetically, it has the same effect."
- Kasi Kaye Iliopoulos

"True spirituality is not taught, it's caught. Once our sails have been unfurled to the Spirit, henceforth our motivation for the journey toward holiness and wholeness is immense gratitude."
- Richard Rohr

"Someone who seems doddery is perhaps not doddery at all but only an older person absorbed in squinting concentration, as though on an ultimate trip, memorizing a scene, grateful for being alive to see it."
- Paul Theroux

"It's up to us to choose contentment and thankfulness now-and to stop imagining that we have to have everything perfect before we'll be happy."
- Joanna Gaines

"Let us not take what we eat for granted; let us view our meals as an opportunity to give our Lord praise."
- Dillon Burroughs

"Find gratitude in the little things and your well of gratitude will never run dry."
- Antonia Montoya

"We tend to forget that happiness doesn't come as a result of getting something we don't have, but rather of recognizing and appreciating what we do have."
- Frederick Keonig

"If we think we will have joy only by praying and singing psalms, we will be disillusioned. But if we fill our lives with simple good things and constantly thank God for them, we will be joyful, that is, full of joy. And what about our problems? When we determine to dwell on the good and excellent things in life, we will be so full of those things that they will tend to swallow our problems."
- Richard J. Foster

"We can only be said to be alive in those moments, where our hearts are conscious of our treasures."
- Thorton Wilder

"Gratitude is the gateway to a positive life."
- A.D. Posey

"Gratitude opens our eyes… We are often praying for something God has already given us."
- Steve Maraboli

"Everyone enjoys being acknowledged and appreciated. Sometimes even the simplest act of gratitude can change someone's entire day. Take the time to recognize and value the people around you and appreciate those who make a difference in your lives."
- Roy T. Bennett

"There is a calmness
to a life lived
in gratitude,
a quiet joy."

Ralph H. Blum

"Were there no God, we would be in this glorious world with grateful hearts, and no one thank."
- **Christina Rossetti**

"Gratitude, the ability to count your blessings, is the ultimate way to connect with the heart."
- **Baptist de Pape**

"Gratitude washes all of my worries and my stress away."
- **Akiroq Brost**

"Then the clarifying thing happens, and what you need to do, what you must do, is not a question, not demand more revelation than what is given, be quiet in the face of it, quiet and grateful that it has been given to you to see this, to be for even a short time aware of the extraordinary layered depths and profound beauty of the world to which we mostly blind ourselves."
- **Dean Koontz**

"In the moments we are awake to the wonder of simply being alive, gratitude flows, no matter our circumstances."
- **M.J. Ryan**

"Not what we say about our blessings, but how we use them, is the true measure of our thanksgiving."
- W.T. Purkiser

"Social scientists have found that the fastest way to feel happiness is to practice gratitude."
- Chip Conley

"Gratitude pours forth continually, as if the unexpected had just happened-the gratitude of a convalescent-for convalescence was unexpected....
The rejoicing of strength that is returning, of a reawakened faith in a tomorrow and the day after tomorrow, of a sudden sense and anticipation of a future, of impending adventures, of seas that are open again."
- Friedrich Nietzsche

"The less approval I get, the more chances I have to develop a relationship with my inner sense of approval. Thankless environments are actually useful for this. They help me discover my own thankfulness and my own self-appreciation."
- Vironika Tugaleva

"Love and gratitude offers courage."
- Auliq-Ice

"Morning Short List: 1. Woke up √ 2. Air to breath √
3. Food to eat √ 4. Roof over head √
...yep, it's a Good day!"
- **Russell Kyle**

"Want what you have, and then you can
have what you want."
- **Frederick Dodson**

"If having a soul means being able to feel love
and loyalty and gratitude, then animals are
better off than a lot of humans."
- **James Herriot**

"If you want to turn your life around, try
thankfulness. It will change your life mightily."
- **Gerald Good**

"Thank God I have seen an orange sky with purple
clouds. How easy it is to forget that we have the
privilege of living in God's art gallery."
- **Erica Goros**

"Behind every creative act is a statement of love.
Every artistic creation is a statement of gratitude."
- **Kilroy J. Oldster**

"When you are grateful, fear disappears
and abundance appears."
- Anthony Robbins

"God has two dwellings; one in heaven, and the
other in a meek and thankful heart."
- Izaak Walton

"If we want to keep the blessings of life coming to us,
we must learn to be grateful for whatever is given."
- Harold Klemp

"Thankfulness creates gratitude which generates
contentment that causes peace."
- Todd Stocker

"I am thankful to all the souls,
I meet in the journey of life."
- Lailah Gifty Akita

"I have always found a mere 'thank you' an
insufficient expression that makes my voice
sound miserly and ungrateful."
- Susan Abulhawa

"On a second note, though, I have something to say about pain. There are lots of kinds of pain. Pain of smashing your fingers in a car door, pains of losing a baby, pain of failing a test. But in their own little ways, these pains are all agonizing. Which is sad, and yet, happy, if you really think about it. If we never lost our car keys, or stepped in gum, or had a bad hair day, what kind of people would we be? In a word? Boring. We wouldn't be passionate; we wouldn't know it was exciting to get pregnant, or score an A on a final. So that's why, today at least, I am grateful for pain. Because it's part of what makes me the whacky, goofy, jaded, person that I am. Peace."
- Alysha Speer

"Cultivate the habit of being grateful for every good thing that comes to you, and to give thanks continuously. And because all things have contributed to your advancement, you should include all things in your gratitude."
- Ralph Waldo Emerson

"The path to enlightenment is when you allow presence, love and gratitude to overlap your ego."
- Matthew Donnelly

"There is a calmness
to a life lived
in gratitude,
a quiet joy."

Ralph H. Blum

"Gratitude also opens your eyes to the limitless potential of the universe, while dissatisfaction closes your eyes to it."
- **Stephen Richards**

"Be thankful to those who refuse to help you, for they force you to summon upon your warrior within."
- **Miya Yamanouchi**

"I can write three hundred and sixty-five grateful thanks. Cultivate the habit to write gratitude daily."
- **Lailah Gifty Akita**

"The more grateful we are, the more we practice this in our everyday lives, the more connected we become to the universe around us."
- **Stephen Richards**

"If we magnified blessings as much as we magnify disappointments, we would all be much happier."
- **John Wooden**

"'Thank you' is a wonderful phrase. Use it. It will add stature to your soul."
- **Marjorie Pay Hinckley**

"If forgiveness is medicine for the soul,
then gratitude is vitamins."
- Steve Maraboli

"Children are grateful when Santa Claus puts in their
stockings gifts of toys or sweets. Could I not be
grateful to Santa Claus when he put in my stockings
the gift of two miraculous legs? We thank people for
birthday presents of cigars and slippers. Can I thank
no one for the birthday present of birth?"
- G.K. Chesterton

"Practicing gratitude in the moment of frustration
can really be a game changer."
- Bruce Weinstein

"Smile and Know, Thank and Know, became my
mantra as I went about my days smiling and
knowing when I could. As I did so, I was walking
in complete faith, which left me naturally
wanting to thank as well."
- Bronnie Ware

"As we express our gratitude, we must never forget
that the highest appreciation is not to utter words,
but to live by them."
- John F. Kennedy

"If you do believe in God, and your first instinct
in all things must be gratitude: for creation,
or love, for mercy."
- **Jonathan V. Last**

"I want for people not to worry so much. Life ain't
going to be perfect, but things will work out. People
come to visit and I always tell them not to worry. If
you got something to eat, don't worry, be grateful.
Just look at all those books. Those books aren't about
food. They're to do with worrying about food."
- **George Dawson**

"In spite of his painful encounters with the world
and its problems, Solomon does not recommend
either pessimism or cynicism. Rather, he admonishes
us to be realistic about life, accept God's gifts and
enjoy them. He advises us to trust God and
enjoy what we do have rather than complain
about what we don't have."
- **Warren W. Wiersbe**

"He has seen enough of daily evil to be thankful
for small goods that come his way."
- **Bernard Pomerance**

"His gratitude widened his smile and bent his back."
- **Arundhati Roy**

"The very joyful thing about seeing ourselves and life from a place of gratitude instead of entitlement- is that this way of breathing allows us to be forgiving of difficult circumstances in life and of those people who delivered such difficult circumstances to us. Gratitude allows us second chances at joy; not with the same circumstances or those same people; but it alleviates the burden of bitterness that comes with not receiving what one believes he/she was entitled to have. We can instead look forward into life and see that there will be many good things and we will be grateful for them."
- C. JoyBell C.

"Grace isn't a little prayer you chant before receiving a meal. It's a way to live."
- Jacqueline Winspear

"I count myself lucky, having long ago won a lottery paid to me in seven sunrises a week for life."
- Robert Brault

"In a world where thrushes sing and willow trees are golden in the spring, boredom should have been included among the seven deadly sins."
- Elizabeth Goudge

"The reason that so many fail to find happiness is that they fail to find gratitude."

Rasheed Ogunlaru

"Both joy and gratitude go hand in hand together.
More grateful you are more joyful you will be."
- Vishwas Chavan

"And when I give thanks for the seemingly
microscopic, I make a place for
God to grow within me."
- Ann Voskamp

"Wherever you are, be there with love. Be there with
compassion, kindness, and gratitude.
Smile and show you care."
- Debasish Mridha

"There are only two ways to live your life.
One is as though nothing is a miracle. The other
is as though everything is a miracle."
- Albert Einstein

"Embrace the change you desperately need.
Tear down your walls and show
gratitude for little things."
- J. Loren Norris

"I have been finding treasures in places I did not want to search. I have been hearing wisdom from tongues I did not want to listen. I have been finding beauty where I did not want to look. And I have learned so much from journeys I did not want to take. Forgive me, O Gracious One; for I have been closing my ears and eyes for too long. I have learned that miracles are only called miracles because they are often witnessed by only those who can can see through all of life's illusions. I am ready to see what really exists on other side, what exists behind the blinds, and taste all the ugly fruit instead of all that looks right, plump and ripe."
- Suzy Kassem

"Gratitude paints little smiley faces on everything it touches."
- Richelle E. Goodrich

"The most important and most significant good quality in our human life is gratitude. Unfortunately, that good quality we somehow manage not to express either in our thoughts or in our actions. Right from the beginning of our life, we have somehow learned not to express it. So we have the least amount of the very thing that we need most in order to become a better person."
- Sri Chinmoy

"Tough times don't last always. Your hard times are there to shape you and develop your character. It causes you to become more aware of life and you develop an attitude of gratitude. Don't lose hope because it gets better."
- **Amaka Imani Nkosazana**

"When our perils are past, shall our gratitude sleep?"
- **George Canning**

"Love yourself first to fill your heart with bliss. Now give it away with humility, love, and gratitude."
- **Debasish Mridha**

"If you appreciate, you will appreciate."
- **Bernard Kelvin Clive**

"Feeling grateful to breathe a new day. Gratitude is a way to submit to the flow of life."
- **Vishwas Chavan**

"The roots of all goodness lie in the soil of appreciation for goodness."
- **Dalai Lama**

"Once a day, stop whatever you are doing and notice 2 things that you are grateful for in your situation or circumstance and in your physical space. Make a habit of this and truly expand your heart to receiving more to be grateful for. There is more than enough reason to feel grateful always; acknowledge that and where possible, give thanks for it."
- Malti Bhojwani

"Gratitude means to recognize the good in your life, be thankful for whatever you have, some people may not even have one of those things you consider precious to you (love, family, friends etc). Each day give thanks for the gift of life. You are blessed"
- Pablo

"When you overlook the small blessings in your life, chances are that no amount of blessings would ever make you happy."
- Edmond Mbiaka

"You have become more and therefore expect more, but never become too purpose-driven to step back and realize just how far you have progressed."
- Chris Matakas

"Gratitude
is not just a word;
it is a way a of life."

Rob Martin

"The whole purpose of education is to create a window of the mind through which you can see the world. Look through that window with your own profound love, joy, harmony, and gratitude."
- Debasish Mridha

"Don't waste all today worrying about the possible mistakes you may have made yesterday. You don't know what will happen tomorrow or how long we have here, so enjoy what you have today since you have it. May you be thankful for today and live it to the fullest as it truly is a gift"
- Angie Karan

"Gratitude begins in our hearts and then dovetails into behavior. It almost always makes you willing to be of service, which is where the joy resides. It means that you are willing to stop being such a jerk. When you are aware of all that has been given to you, in your lifetime and the past few days, it is hard not to be humbled, and pleased to give back."
- Anne Lamott

"One may suffer the long-term in order to grow in appreciation for the small things. For in short-term suffering, one only notices the large."
- Criss Jami

"God will bring you a gift. However, it is up to you to stop shaking the same box and expecting something wonderful will fall out of it again. After a while, you are going to break that box and it won't remind you of that moment when it meant everything to you."
- **Shannon L. Alder**

"Gratitude shouldn't be an occasional incident but a continuous attitude."
- **Anthony Nyuiemedy-Adiase**

"(Some people) have a wonderful capacity to appreciate again and again, freshly and naively, the basic goods of life, with awe, pleasure, wonder, and even ecstasy."
- **A.H. Maslow**

"Saying thanks to the world, and acknowledging your own accomplishments, is a great way to feel good and stay positive."
- **Rachel Robins**

"Gratitude is a divine emotion. It fills the heart, not to bursting; it warms it, but not to fever. I like to taste leisurely of bliss. Devoured in haste, I do not know its flavor."
- **Charlotte Brontë**

"Cicero said that 'gratitude is not only the greatest
of virtues, but the parent of all others.' If that's true,
then my happiness does not cause me to be grateful
for what I have. My gratitude for what I have
causes me to be happy. Gratitude births
the virtue of happiness."
- Jennifer Dukes Lee

"There are two days in the year that you cannot
do anything: Yesterday & Tomorrow:
Only Today you can Be Happy, Smile,
Dream, Love, Feel, & Be Thankful…"
- Dalai Lama

"Today is a beautiful day. Thank you!"
- Ron Barrow

"People rarely get more of anything until they have
learned to be grateful for what they already have."
- Michael Hyatt

"No one who achieves success does so without the
help of others. The wise and confident acknowledge
this help with gratitude."
- Alfred North Whitehead

"Never kill your 'What if's",
first be grateful for 'What is'."
- **Drishti Bablani**

"In normal life we hardly realize how much more we receive than we give, and life cannot be rich without such gratitude. It is so easy to overestimate the importance of our own achievements compared with what we owe to the help of others."
- **Dietrich Bonhoeffer**

"Gratitude is the payment for what
we have received. It also opens our hearts
to fill our lives with abundance."
- **Debasish Mridha**

"How simple it is to acknowledge that all the worry in the world could not control the future. How simple it is to see that we can only be happy now, and that there will never be a time
when it is not now."
- **Jonathan Harnisch**

"Superficial social niceties are far different from the deep emotion of thanksgiving."
- **Alexandra Katehakis**

"I would maintain that thanks are the
highest form of thought, and that gratitude
is happiness doubled by wonder."
- G.K. Chesterton

"Throughout the day, anytime you find yourself
feeling stressed or wanting to complain, stop for
10 seconds and breathe. Count your breaths
and your blessings."
- Jon Gordon

"Mamma says gratitude helps us to see
what is there instead of what isn't."
- Annette Bridges

"When we raise the feeling of gratitude
and appreciation for who we are,
we know we are at Home."
- Raphael Zernoff

"Find magic in the little things, and the big things
you always expected will start to show up."
- Isa Zapata

"Extending gratitude to another says, "I see
what you've done and I thank you for
the energy you put forth."
- Molly Friedenfeld

"Gratitude and attitude are not challenges; they are choices."

Robert Braathe

"A sincere attitude of gratitude is a beatitude for secured altitudes. Appreciate what you have been given and you will be promoted higher."
- **Israelmore Ayivor**

"[The most fortunate are those who] have a wonderful capacity to appreciate again and again, freshly and naively, the basic goods of life, with awe, pleasure, wonder, and even ecstasy."
– **Abraham Maslow**

"Happiness is in contentment, gratitude, and love. It is a lifestyle, not a location."
- **Ogwo David Emenike**

"Everything we encounter can have a positive influence in shaping our life when we adopt a lens of Gratitude."
- **Rob Martin**

"Life is not a maze where you have your eyes on the gaps, life is a beautiful journey, stop looking for the gaps."
- **Malti Bhojwani**

"Things turn out best for people who make the best of the way things turn out."
- John Wooden

"While the classic conversion story involves desperation, hitting bottom, and a plea for help, I think now that it was gratitude, as well as the suffering I'd seen, that made room for me to open my heart to something new."
- Sara Miles

"I love the life that living not because I have achieved all my dreams, but because I am very grateful for every little blessing in my life. I grew up hearing that 'half a loaf of bread is better than none'."
- Edmond Mbiaka

"When my parents were liberated, four years before I was born, they found that the ordinary world outside the camp had been eradicated. There was no more simple meal, nothing was less than extraordinary: a fork, a mattress, a clean shirt, a book. Not to mention such things that can make one weep: an orange, meat and vegetables, hot water. There was no ordinariness to return to, no refuge from the blinding potency of things, an apple screaming its sweet juice."
- Anne Michaels

"The highest form of education teaches us to find
the truth by searching with love,
harmony, and gratitude."
- Debasish Mridha

"Gratitude also opens your eyes to the limitless
potential of the universe, while dissatisfaction
closes your eyes to it."
- Stephen Richards

"It is a great thing to be young and to live without
pain. And yet it is a blessing few of us count
until we lose it."
- Geraldine Brooks

"I can and will improve the world. I will smile, show
kindness, and be grateful. I refuse to be unhappy."
- Richelle E. Goodrich

"You need to be able to find hope in your
circumstances. We need it for ourselves and
our children. Laurie and I both believe that when
we reflect on all that we have and all that we love
and all that we are thankful for, we feel
that hope and that peace."
- Laura Lane

"Not only the footwear, wear also the courtesy,
respect, and gratitude in your heart
while stepping out of home."
- **Rupali Desai**

"It is not what happens to you or for you that makes
you grateful. It's how you respond to what is
happening, that shows your belief about gratitude."
- **Sumner Davenport**

"They both seemed to understand that describing it
was beyond their powers, the gratitude that spreads
through your body when a burden gets lifted, and
the sense of homecoming that follows, when you
suddenly remember what it feels like to be yourself."
- **Tom Perrotta**

"Do not spoil what you have by desiring what you
have not; remember that what you now have was
once among the things you only hoped for."
– **Epicurus**

"Life is both beautiful and painful. In whatever
situation we find ourselves in, no matter how
unfortunate it may seem, there is always something
to be thankful for – if we only choose to see it."
- **Frederick Espiritu**

"Whatever you
appreciate
and give thanks for
will increase
in your life."

Sanaya Roman

"You say grace before meals. All right. But I say grace before the concert and the opera, and grace before the play and pantomime, and grace before I open a book, and grace before sketching, painting, swimming, fencing, boxing, walking, playing, dancing and grace before I dip the pen in the ink."
- G. K. Chesterton

"If you count all your assets,
you always show a profit."
- Robert Quillen

"If I spend every moment, for the rest of my days,
thanking God for all his goodness to us,
that would still not be enough."
- Johanna Spyri

"Sometimes it takes a little jolt to make us
appreciate what we've got."
- Robert Hellenga

"Charlie Brown: 'A penny! Rats! Why couldn't I have found a nickel? What good is a penny these days? Why do things like that always happen to me?!' *walks off frustrated* Lucy: 'Gee, he found a penny! Why don't things like that ever happen to me?'"
- Charles M. Schulz

"If you never learned the lesson of thankfulness,
begin now. Sum up your mercies; see what
provision God has made for your happiness,
what opportunities for your usefulness,
and what advantages for your success."
- Ida S. Taylor

"Expecting gratitude for a gift is... unseemly."
- Jack Caldwell

"Joy is the net of love by which we can capture souls.
God loves the person who gives with joy. Whoever
gives with joy gives more. The best way to show our
gratitude to God and to people is to accept with joy."
- Mother Teresa

"Dear World, I am excited to be alive in you,
and I am thankful for another year."
- Charlotte Eriksson

"An aware heart is a grateful heart."
- Toni Sorenson

"The Greeks were realists. They saw the beauty of
common things and were content with it."
- Edith Hamilton

"The greatest wisdom is in simplicity. Love, respect, tolerance, sharing, gratitude, forgiveness. It's not complex or elaborate. The real knowledge is free. It's encoded in your DNA. All you need is within you. Great teachers have said that from the beginning. Find your heart, and you will find your way."
- Carlos Barrios

"The moment that you give gratitude is the moment that you find happiness. The moment that you lose gratitude your happiness will vanish and slip through your fingers"
- Rasheed Ogunlaru

"The focus of Thanksgiving should be a reflection of how our lives have been made so much more comfortable by the sacrifices of those who have come before us."
– Emmons

"Grow in a way without losing much of our inner childlike deep senses embracing truthful, pure, simple relief of appreciation and gratitude."
- Angelica Hopes

"I am grateful for the grace to see, to hear, to talk, to feel, to smell, to taste and to walk."
- Lailah Gifty Akita

"Paying tax should be framed as a glorious
civic duty worthy of gratitude
- not a punishment for making money."
- Alain de Botton

"Thank you is the best prayer that anyone could say.
I say that one a lot. Thank you expresses extreme
gratitude, humility, understanding."
- Alice Walker

"The problem that we have with a victim mentality is
that we forget to see the blessings of the day. Because
of this, our spirit is poisoned instead of nourished."
- Steve Maraboli

"Gratitude is the creative force, the mother and father
of love. It is in gratitude that real love exists. Love
expands only when gratitude is there. Limited love
does not offer gratitude. Limited love is immediately
bound by something- by constant desires or constant
demands. But when it is unlimited love, constant
love, then gratitude comes to the fore. This love
becomes all gratitude."
- Sri Chinmoy

"Seesth thou a man that isn't grateful?
He is a great fool."
- Pastor Erukeoghene Taunu Pet

"Whisper sweetly the tenderness of the moment. Let the love teach you the true meaning and passion of this experience we share. With gratitude and reverence for the blessings and miracles I receive and witness, my heart still beats as the little things die to be reborn with a greater joy for life in each moment."
- Jennifer Hillman

"Success depends on your attitude; happiness depends on your gratitude."
- Debasish Mridha

"Feeling gratitude and not expressing it is like wrapping a present and not giving it."
- William Arthur Ward

"Gratitude was never a noun; it's secretly a verb. It is not a place you accept defeat, settle in for broken dreams or call it the best life will get. Gratitude is getting out of laziness, self-pity, denial and insecurity, in order to walk through that door God has been holding open for you this entire time."
- Shannon L. Alder

"Let gratitude be your pure prayer."
- Debasish Mridha

"I am so grateful for the many times God has shown me the mercy of not giving me what I want."

Steve Maraboli

"The unthankful heart… discovers no mercies; but let the thankful heart sweep through the day and, as the magnet finds the iron, so it will find, in every hour, some heavenly blessings!"
- **Henry Ward Beecher**

"I try hard to hold fast to the truth that a full and thankful heart cannot entertain great conceits. When brimming with gratitude, one's heartbeat must surely result in outgoing love, the finest emotion we can ever know."
- **Bill W.**

"Don't get caught in the trap of always "Needing" something. Needing something always projects mind into the future as if you have it and is the opposite of gratitude. Be content in the present moment."
- **Matthew Donnelly**

"We don't truly appreciate what we have until it's gone… We don't really appreciate something until we have experienced some events; we don't really appreciate our parents until we ourselves have become parents. Be grateful for what you have now, and nothing should be taken for granted."
- **Roy T. Bennett**

"I'm grateful for past betrayals, heartaches, and challenges... I thought they were breaking me; but they were sculpting me."
- Steve Maraboli

"The aim of life is appreciation; there is no sense in not appreciating things; and there is no sense in having more of them if you have less appreciation of them."
- G.K. Chesterton

"Hem your blessings with thankfulness so they don't unravel."
- Unknown

"Acknowledging the good that you already have in your life is the foundation for all abundance."
- Eckhart Tolle

"They both seemed to understand that describing it was beyond their powers, the gratitude that spreads through your body when a burden gets lifted, and the sense of homecoming that follows, when you suddenly remember what it feels like to be yourself."
- Tom Perrotta

"Breath is the finest gift of nature.
Be grateful for this wonderful gift."
- Amit Ray

"Gratitude for all the beauty and blessings that we
already enjoy fills our lives with abundance."
- Debasish Mridha

"Gratitude means thankfulness, counting your
blessings, noticing simple pleasures, and
acknowledging everything that you receive. It means
learning to live your life as if everything were a
miracle, and being aware on a continuous basis of
how much you've been given."
- Marelisa Fábrega

"Be thankful for what you have; you'll end up having
more. If you concentrate on what you don't have, you
will never, ever have enough."
- Oprah Winfrey

"A thankful heart is the key to overflowing joy."
- Human Angels

"Gratitude is the real treasure God wants us to find,
because it isn't the pot of gold but the rainbow
that colors our world."
- Richelle E. Goodrich

"Gratitude is a quality similar to electricity:
it must be produced and discharged and
used up in order to exist at all."
–William Faulkner

"You will never accept gratitude as a solution to your
problems, until you have reached the last
stage of grief-acceptance."
- Shannon L. Alder

"But the value of gratitude does not consist solely in
getting you more blessings in the future. Without
gratitude you cannot long keep from dissatisfied
thought regarding things as they are."
- Wallace Wattles

"Perhaps gratitude and love are one and the same."
- Erica Goros

"Gratitude is a 'nice' habit to adopt, warming
your heart and all, but the Kumbaya effect is just the
beginning. Gratefulness goes wayyyyyyy beyond
the momentary feeling good, offering plenty of
long-term and "practical" benefits we
may never have intuited."
- Kelly Corbet

"Happy are those
who value
what they have,
when they have it."

Tammy Rosenfeld

"When I think of how many people in this world have it worse than I do, I realize just how blessed I really am...and I have to give thanks ..."
- Shannan Lea

"Gratitude makes blessings permanent."
- Raheel Farooq

"I made cranberry sauce, and when it was done put it into a dark blue bowl for the beautiful contrast. I was thinking, doing this, about the old ways of gratitude: Indians thanking the deer they'd slain, grace before supper, kneeling before bed. I was thinking that gratitude is too much absent in our lives now, and we need it back, even if it only takes the form of acknowledging the blue of a bowl against the red of cranberries."
- Elizabeth Berg

"It is literally true, as the thankless say, that they have nothing to be thankful for. He who sits by the fire, thankless for the fire, is just as if he had no fire. Nothing is possessed save in appreciation, of which thankfulness is the indispensable ingredient. But a thankful heart hath a continual feast."
- W.J. Cameron

"Can you see the holiness in those things you take for granted–a paved road or a washing machine? If you concentrate on finding what is good in every situation, you will discover that your life will suddenly be filled with gratitude, a feeling that nurtures the soul." - Rabbi Harold Kushner

"Love is such a deep gratitude. When you are truly in love with life, every breath you take is gratitude."
- Bryant McGill

"That's what I learned. I learned I couldn't shed light on love other than to feel its comings and goings and be grateful."
- Diane Keaton

"The highest tribute to the dead is not grief but gratitude."
- Thornton Wilder

"… two different kinds of Japanese psychotherapies, one based on getting people to stop using feelings as an excuse for their actions and the other based on getting people to practice gratitude."
- Will Schwalbe

"Qualifications or not, without gratitude you are not qualified enough to be a leader."
- Unarine Ramaru

"I am grateful to those who have betrayed me...
They thought they were just stabbing me in the back,
but they were also cutting me free
from their poisonous life."
- Steve Maraboli

"As a flower expresses thanks with her beauty and
fragrance for her magnificent life, let us express our
gratitude to every friend with our service and love
and to the Earth for her hospitality and care.
Let us be thankful and let us express the
deepest gratitude for our magnificent life."
- Debasish Mridha

"But studies show that consistently keeping track of
what you are thankful for and acting on those
feelings of appreciation can not only make you
happier, but actually boost your immune system
and keep you healthier."
- Catherine Jessen

"Another thing we can learn to do is to be more
grateful for every day we have with our children.
None of us ever knows how long we have on Earth,
so it is imperative that we live and love
each moment we have."
- Laura Lane

"Showing a little bit of gratitude for a gift is often as difficult as hiding the fact one doesn't like it. Best bit might be your smile."
- Isabella Koldras

"Gratitude bestows reverence.....changing forever how we experience life and the world."
- John Milton

"Let us express our gratitude to those people who make our journeys in life beautiful, easy, and interesting. They are the angels of Eden whom we often forget to appreciate."
- Debasish Mridha

"A grateful mindset can set you free from the prison of disempowerment and the shackles of misery."
- Steve Maraboli

"Be grateful. Not Hateful."
- John A. Passaro

"At times our own light goes out and is rekindled by a spark from another person. Each of us has cause to think with deep gratitude of those who have lighted the flame within us."
- Albert Schweitzer

"Appreciation can change a day, even change a life.
Your willingness to put it into words
is all that is necessary."
- **Margaret Cousins**

"Cultivate and nurture being grateful for every good
thing that comes to you, and to give thanks
continuously. Remembering that In daily life we
must see that it is not happiness that makes us
grateful, but gratefulness that makes us happy."
- **Angie Karan**

"Only unconditional grace can transform a hardened
heart into a grateful heart. Only a free gift can
demolish any notion of quid pro quo. Only an utterly
merciful act of love can fashion
a new creation capable of love."
- **Mark Galli**

"Those who complain much get little,
those who complain little get much."
- **Jeanette Coron**

"Gratitude can transform common days into
thanksgivings, turn routine jobs into joy and change
ordinary opportunities into blessings."
- **William Arthur Ward**

"Don't let your
'future success'
dim the beauty and light
that's in front of you
right now."

Taryn Garland

"I am still searching for a popular prayer which doesn't seek materialistic or other benefits from God and is a simple prayer which simply expresses gratitude in Him and believes what He does will be for our best..."
- **Neelam Saxena Chandra**

"I am so grateful for the many times God has shown me the mercy of not giving me what I want."
- **Steve Maraboli**

"God gave you a gift of 86,400 seconds today. Have you used one to say 'thank you'?"
- **William Arthur Ward**

"Don't let your 'future success' dim the beauty and light that's in front of you right now."
- **Taryn Garland**

"Always be thankful for what you had, what you have, and what you will have in the future."
- **Edmond Mbiaka**

"Happiness is itself a kind of gratitude."
- **Joseph Wood Krutch**

"Truth is, life is going shake you, it will
rip you right out of your comfort zone; just when you
feel settled, it will shock you with some trauma and
make you face adversity in the most undesirable of
ways... And here is the question of it all? What's it all
for... Not many search long enough to know but the
wise ask you. Are you going to be a slave to your
journey or the pioneer to your dream, if God handed
you a lesson; he knew before your time, your
strength could endure; so next time you doubt
another thought or feed your heart with
negative emotions think about it... You are here,
alive, breathing and if that's not enough, then you
should think about what is."
- Nikki Rowe

"The high road of gratitude will get you somewhere
a whole lot faster than the freeway of entitlement."
- James Allen Proctor

"When one has a grateful heart, life is so beautiful."
- Roy T. Bennett

"Just an observation: it is impossible to be both
grateful and depressed. Those with a grateful
mindset tend to see the message in the mess. And
even though life may knock them down, the grateful
find reasons, if even small ones, to get up."
- Steve Maraboli

"Gratitude does not mean the absence of solitude, but the presence of a positive attitude in spite of."
- Gift Gugu Mona

"Sometimes the word 'gratitude' feels too thin to explain things."
- Dee Williams

"Begin each day with a positive thought and a grateful heart."
- Roy Bennett

"Silence your mind and breathe. Take this moment to show gratitude for the abundance of blessings in your life."
- Karen A. Baquiran

"You pray in your distress and in your need; would that you might pray also in the fullness of your joy and in your days of abundance."
- Kahlil Gibran

"For a wise man, I have been told, once said, 'Gratitude is best and most effective when it does not evaporate in empty phrases.' But alas, my lady, I am but a mass of empty phrases, it would seem."
- Isaac Asimov

"The greatest of blessings can come from what appear to be the smallest and most insignificant of things. Don't discredit anything or anyone. One person, one tiny thing, one little shift can change your life in enormous ways."
- **Patience W. Smith**

"The moment one gives close attention to anything, even a blade of grass, it becomes a mysterious, awesome, indescribably magnificent world in itself."
- **Henry Miller**

"I look back upon my youth and realize how so many people gave me help, understanding, courage – very important things to me – and they never knew it. They entered into my life and became powers within me. All of us live spiritually by what others have given us, often unwittingly, in the significant hours of our life. At the time these significant hours may not even be perceived. We may not recognize them until years later when we look back, as one remembers some long-ago music or a boyhood landscape. We all owe to others much of the gentleness and wisdom that we have made our own; and we may well ask ourselves what will others owe to us."
- **Albert Schweitzer**

"We have so much
for what to be grateful
and if we thank for it,
we will have
even much more."

Victoria Vorel

"'Be grateful for the things you don't have that you don't want.' -Bob Dylan's Dad"
- **Bob Dylan**

"Gratitude is one of the strongest pillars of a happy life."
- **Edmond Mbiaka**

"If there is one thing the psychic taught me, it's that people and events are rarely who and what we think they are. They are more meaningful, more worth our attention-part of some finely choreographed, eternal dance that we would be wise to bow down before in gratitude and humility."
- **Leslie Morgan Steiner**

"There are still blue skies and rainbows and days bathed in sunlight. There are colorful shade trees filled with sweet bird songs. And there are wishing stars in the heavens as well as angels in God's service. So, lift up your eyes. Refuse to be unhappy."
- **Richelle E. Goodrich**

"A generous heart filled with gratitude is a magnet for abundance."
- **Debasish Mridha**

"The fact that you woke up this morning is proof
that this day has already been
predetermined in your favor."
- Russell Kyle

"It seems The Adversary needs neither their guilt nor
their request, but simply their return. In other words,
since repentance is the process whereby guilt is
turned into gratitude, He doesn't mind if they skip
a step and go directly to gratitude."
- Geoffrey Wood

"This world is not a wonderful place where
unfortunately many evil things happen; but this
world is a terrible place where fortunately many
miracles and other wonderful things happen."
- C. JoyBell C.

"I may not be where I want to be but I'm thankful for
not being where I used to be."
- Joyce Meyer

"The road to happiness starts with a deep breath
and an awareness of the many blessings
tied to that single breath."
- Richelle E. Goodrich

"Peace starts within. We are what we give."
- **Sal Di Leo**

"I would maintain that thanks are the highest form of thought; and that gratitude is happiness doubled by wonder."
- **G.K. Chesterton**

"One minute of sincere gratitude can wash away a lifetime's disappointments."
- **Silvia Hartmann**

"The more you appreciate,
the more you have to appreciate."
- **Carma Spence**

"'Rain don't fall on a with if she doesn't want it to, although personally I prefer to get wet and be thankful.' 'Thankful for what?' said Tiffany. 'That I'll get dry later.'"
- **Terry Pratchett**

"The humanitarian is a treasure hunter seeking gems of remedy and appreciation."
- **Richelle E. Goodrich**

"There is a calmness to a life
lived in gratitude, a quiet joy."
- Ralph H. Blum

"This morning I woke up, how blessed I am. Eyes to
see, a voice to speak. Words to read and love to feel?
If this isn't something to be thankful for,
I'm not sure what is."
- Nikki Rowe

"When we replace a sense of service and gratitude
with a sense of entitlement and expectation, we
quickly see the demise of our relationships,
society, and economy."
- Steve Maraboli

"Ingratitude produces pride while gratitude
produces humility."
- Orrin Woodward

"Being Happy on Purpose is about making a
conscious decision in each moment to move towards
happiness. It is not about a perfect life. It is not about
having things. It is about creating YOUR experience
and being open to the beauty, joy, and abundance
that already exists in your life and calibrating
yourself to recognize it with ease"
- Jennifer Sparks

"And throughout life, I think I would like to walk with more humility and less anger, more love and less fear. I want to walk confidently, but without arrogance. I want to walk in deep appreciation. I want to be genuinely thankful for life's extravagant, yet simple, gifts – a star-splattered night sky or a hot drink on an ice-cold day."
- **Steve Goodier**

"Living your life through Gratitude, is not one of comparing how you are better than someone else; or Gratitude only for what you own or obtain or achieve. Living your life through Gratitude, is seeing that the world would be missing something very valuable if you were not in it."
- **Sumner Davenport**

"Gratefulness is the key to a happy life that we hold in our hands, because if we are not grateful, then no matter how much we have we will not be happy - because we will always want to have something else or something more."
- **Brother David Steindl-Rast**

"When things are bad, be thankful...they are not as bad as they could be."
- **Dixie Waters**

"Appreciation is
a wonderful thing.
It makes what is
excellent in others
belong to us as well."

Voltaire

"To live a life of gratitude is to open our eyes to the countless ways in which we are supported by the world around us."
– Gregg Krech

"If people begin to be more grateful,
they will see the wonders of life."
- Lailah Gifty Akita

"Be consistent in your dedication to showing your gratitude to others. Gratitude is a fuel, a medicine, and spiritual and emotional nourishment."
- Steve Maraboli

"When you are beloved and express gratitude like the fragrance of a beautiful flower, you are happy."
- Debasish Mridha

"Make it a habit to tell people thank you.
To express your appreciation, sincerely and without the expectation of anything in return. Truly appreciate those around you, and you'll soon find many others around you. Truly appreciate life, and you'll find that you have more of it."
- Ralph Marston

"One would like to live poetically, that is,
with gratitude and grace."
- **Marty Rubin**

"No one can obtain felicity by pursuit. This explains
why one of the elements of being happy is the feeling
that a debt of gratitude is owed, a debt impossible to
pay. Now, we do not owe gratitude to ourselves. To
be conscious of gratitude is to acknowledge a gift."
- **Josef Pieper**

"The unthankful heart discovers no mercies; but the
thankful heart will find, in every hour,
some heavenly blessings."
- **Henry Ward Beecher**

"A grateful mind by owing owes not, but still pays,
at once indebted and discharged;
what burden then?"
- **John Milton**

"The will to love, the desire to help,
and an open mind with gratitude can
unlock the door to eternal happiness."
- **Debasish Mridha**

"How would your life be different if you celebrated the things in your life that you do have instead of lamenting things that you don't? Let today be the day you embrace gratitude and appreciation and let go of entitlement and expectation."
- Steve Maraboli

Words & Wisdom Series

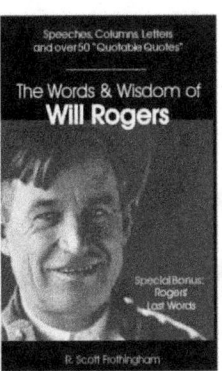

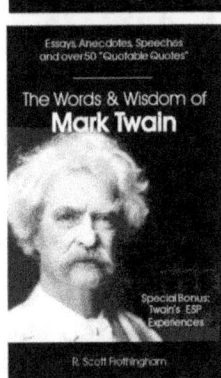

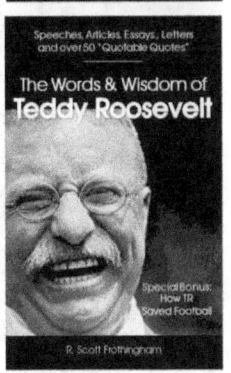

"The Words and Wisdom of" Ben Franklin, Will Rogers, Elbert Hubbard, Dean Smith, Mark Twain, Teddy Roosevelt, and Abraham Lincoln …
… all 7 books available online at retailers of quality books.

www.ingramcontent.com/pod-product-compliance
Lightning Source LLC
Chambersburg PA
CBHW072042280526
45788CB00006B/2157